Praise for *Nurturing Boys*

"With a deemphasis on fragile masculinity, frat boy culture, and everything in between, Nurturing Boys guides parents toward a better understanding of childhood behavior patterns, rather than defaulting to toxic norms."

—**Dr. John Duffy**, author of *Parenting the New Teen in the Age of Anxiety* and *The Available Parent*

"Stuffed full of practical tips for teachers and parents alike, Nurturing Boys will help you connect with, empower, and uplift the young men in your life."

—**Becca Anderson**, author of *Every Day Thankful* and *The Buddha's Guide to Gratitude*

"This is the go-go guide to emotional intelligence for boys; Just excellent."

—**Judy Ford**, author of *Wonderful Ways to Love a Child*

NUTURING BOYS

NUTURING BOYS

200 Ways to Raise a Boy's Emotional Intelligence from Boyhood to Manhood

WILL GLENNON

Foreword by Dr. John Duffy, author of
Parenting the New Teen in the Age of Anxiety

Conari
Press

CORAL GABLES

Published by Mango Publishing Group, a division of Mango Media Inc.

Cover Design: Elina Diaz
Cover Photo/illustration: © goodluz/Adobe Stock, © Syda Productions/
Adobe Stock, © mkitina4/ Adobe Stock, © jbrown/ Adobe Stock
Layout & Design: Elina Diaz

For permission requests, please contact the publisher at:
Mango Publishing Group
2850 S Douglas Road, 2nd Floor
Coral Gables, FL 33134 USA
info@mango.bz

For special orders, quantity sales, course adoptions and corporate sales,
please email the publisher at sales@mango.bz. For trade and wholesale
sales, please contact Ingram Publisher Services at customer.service@
ingramcontent.com or +1.800.509.4887.

Nurturing Boys: 200 Ways to Raise a Boy's Emotional Intelligence from
Boyhood to Manhood

Library of Congress Cataloging-in-Publication number: has been requested
ISBN: (print) 978-1-64250-370-8, (ebook) 978-1-64250-371-5
BISAC category code: FAM034000, FAMILY & RELATIONSHIPS /
Parenting / General

Printed in the United States of America

Foreword

Like Will, I have dedicated my professional life to
researching positive methods of parenting, aiming to
impact the psyche of our children and how they treat
others in the future. So, when Will asked me to craft
a foreword for this book, I reflected upon my own
experience as a young boy in America, as well as the lack
of accessible advice available when I was raising my own
boy. As a clinical psychologist, certified life coach, and,
most importantly, a devoted husband and doting father to
my only son, I have personally experienced the hardships
of raising a boy in our ever-evolving, fast-paced society.
With technology being at the forefront of everything
we do, it seems as if our children are more vulnerable
to succumbing to toxic societal norms, at earlier ages
than *ever*. Although everything around us seems to
be progressing—technology, economies, and trends—
traditional methods of raising our boys have withstood
the test of time, imprinting our sons with the same archaic
notions of toxic masculinity from childhood and onwards.
"Real men don't cry." "Man up!" "Don't be a girl!"
Unfortunately, these are phrases that I, and far too many
other men, have heard consistently since adolescence. So,

how do we reverse this toxic phenomenon if the society we live in seemingly perpetuates its existence? Well, first and foremost, the journey must begin within the very families that are currently raising these young boys.

As parents, I know we all want to nurture and care for our children, protecting them from any semblance of harm at all times. Often, we forget that danger does not solely lurk in a physical form but also within the social norms encouraging toxic masculinity and detaching our sons from their emotional intelligence. By guiding parents toward a healthier, more emotionally literate path of raising young boys, Will's book *Nurturing Boys* tackles an all-too-overlooked issue that impacts nearly half our population. With over two hundred straightforward (and well-researched) methods of showing our boys the importance of nurture by validating and acknowledging their emotions, Will encourages the healthy expression of feelings within our sons through playful parenting techniques. Equipped with the tools provided within this book, parents will be ready to skillfully encourage the emotional management of their boys, navigate constructive, not destructive, utilization of their sons' emotions, and establish a safe space for effective communication. With a deemphasis on fragile masculinity, frat boy culture, and everything in between, *Nurturing Boys* guides parents toward a better understanding of childhood behavior patterns, rather than defaulting to toxic norms. Encompassing thoughtful anecdotal details throughout, Will's book will warmly reach out to you, like the friend who always shares their most successful parenting tips with you over dinner.

This intimate read conveys the solution to a problem that impacts not only our young boys, but also the world we eventually must send them off into. At one point or another, we have each been impacted by the wrath of toxic masculinity. Our current world has been plagued with mass shootings, domestic violence, and male domination due to the violent effects of social norms that deem emotional vulnerability a wretched sin. There is no better time than *now* to put your foot down and demand radical change: a change which seeks to liberate the emotions of young boys and nurture their fragility rather than demonize it. Although it is impossible to control all aspects of the environment we send our children into, what we can control is the approach and methods of parenting we impose upon them. I hope you join me in following the advice and guidance Will provides in this book and have as much fun as I did engaging with my son throughout this experience.

Sincerely,
Dr. John Duffy
Proud husband of Julie and father to George

CHAPTER 1

The Importance of Emotionally Healthy Sons

When my son was five, I took him on one of many trips to visit his grandparents. As we sat around in the post–evening meal glow, I watched him work the room in his unique and extraordinary style. He had a capacity to insert himself effortlessly right into your heart, alternately playing, talking, touching, cuddling, laughing, and hugging. As he made his rounds before being shuttled off to bed, my mother, who sat beside me watching this unfold, turned to me and said, "He reminds me so much of you at that age."

She meant it as a compliment, both for him and for me, but it left me speechless—I could not ever remember myself so uninhibitedly connected to my heart. Somehow, in the process of growing up male in this culture, in the space of a decade between my childhood and my confused teenage years, I had grown into a young man who lived completely within his head and was, without even knowing it, completely cut off from his feelings.

The long journey back to reconnecting with my emotional self has been the most difficult and painful thing I have ever undertaken, and the years I existed as an emotional cripple are lost forever. Watching my son, who was not yet weighted down by the enormous pressure to be tough, to be rational, to hold back tears, and, implicitly, to stop feeling, I vowed that I would do whatever was necessary to help him survive his youth with his beautiful heart intact. It was a solemn promise I made that day, but not one that was easy to achieve. Much of whatever wisdom might appear in this book arose from mistakes I made with him.

As a society, we have made great strides on behalf of women, and that is an extraordinary thing. We have realized that in denigrating the feminine, we have impoverished the whole. By systematically hindering women from assuming their power in the world, we have lost generations of insight. And in the process, we have forced our sons to grow into adulthood without access to the very resources they need to become decent, caring, full human beings.

We look out today in horror at a society scarred by senseless violence and hatred. From mindless massacres in our schools to the numbing randomness of street violence, our society seems to have taken leave of its senses. And the truth that we scarcely want to admit is that the violence is virtually all committed by men, and these men were once young boys who laughed and hugged and loved.

Our focus on the plight of women has produced a significant body of research on the how, when, and why of collapsing self-esteem in girls. Though we have only begun to turn our attention toward the development of boys, some significant information has emerged. Studies show that young girls tend to be strong and self-confident until the onset of puberty. It is then that the crisis of self-esteem hits and hits hard. Boys, on the other hand, tend to go through two distinct crises: the first at age five or six, and the second at puberty. One more tantalizing piece of information is that among infants and toddlers, boys tend to be more emotionally expressive than girls, only to lose this skill as they grow. At age five or six, the acculturation process first kicks in, and for our sons, it kicks in with a merciless impact.

As I see it, the issue in raising our daughters is providing them with the love, support, internal strength, and self-confidence to grow fully into their lives; the issue for our sons is bringing them to maturity with their emotional centers intact and accessible.

Through interactions at school and on the playground and exposure to cultural stereotypes in television shows, movies, and video games, our sons quickly learn that boys are expected to be tough, showing no other emotions except anger. In a boy's world, everything becomes competitive, and you need to take the blows—literally and figuratively—and pretend they don't hurt if you hope to measure up. At age five, boys are already deep into the process of sealing off their hearts, cutting the ties that connect them to their own emotional worlds.

The second and potentially more dangerous crisis strikes boys at puberty, when issues as emotionally charged as sex, love, and one's identity as a man suddenly emerge with urgency. Yet the very resources our sons need to deal with these issues, a solid grounding in their own emotional worlds, never fully developed. As a consequence, they find themselves living in a strange and dangerous world filled with pressing and confusing questions, and they don't even have the language to find the answers.

Cut off from their emotions, our sons are truly lost, since they do not even know what is missing. They try to compensate by pressing on to understand, to develop their gift of reason, for therein appears to lie protection from the unknown. Their emotions remain intact but are repressed into the darkness of their unconscious.

Much research still needs to be done to complete the picture. One question that may not be answered for a very long time is just how much of the behavioral differences between boys and girls is rooted in biology and how much is a product of social and cultural expectations. At one extreme are those who believe that boys and girls are from different worlds altogether—for lack of a better term, the "Mars and Venus" theory. I personally think this is a foolhardy position, if for no other reason than it tells us to stop thinking and worrying about how we raise our children; the results are inevitably coded into our genes.

But the status quo is not acceptable. Raising generation after generation of girls with shattered self-esteem and boys with little or no emotional intelligence is neither inevitable nor desirable. There is nothing "alien" about little boys or little girls. We are the same species and we dream the same dreams. We all want to love and be loved and to have lives of meaning and purpose. While we cannot change our biology, we can begin to change the way we raise our children.

In my earlier book, *200 Ways to Raise a Girl's Self-Esteem*, I tried to provide practical suggestions for giving our daughters a better chance of growing up with their self-esteem not only intact but vibrantly strong and resilient. In this book I offer equally straightforward suggestions for helping our sons grow into manhood

connected to their hearts and resonating with the deep
emotional intelligence that they will need to live full and
joyful lives. Some are suggestions to develop or support
your son's emotional repertoire; others are attitudes that
we adults must cultivate in order to nurture our boys
into adulthood. No matter who the boy in your life is, no
matter his age, it's never too late to start.

CHAPTER 2

Exploring Your Own Assumptions

Living at a time of great transformation is exciting, especially when the changes taking place are long overdue and coming at a dizzying pace. But it is also extremely challenging since, as pioneers of change, we are constantly entering new territory in which we have only a general idea of which direction to take. It takes enormous energy and focus to sort out the paths and to figure out what we need to do to make this journey easier for our sons. But most of us are more than willing to commit this energy and time because we want to provide our sons with full, rich upbringings that will serve as a solid foundation for their growth and development into the extraordinary men we know they can be.

By far the most difficult part of our task is discovering and dismantling the places where our own training hinders

our role as pioneers. Someone must go first, and it is both
a great honor and a solemn responsibility, but we need to
remember that our own training, our own complex array
of assumptions, was forged under different times. Much
of it is no longer appropriate for or supportive of our
immediate task.

Simply replaying past expectations, assumptions, and
traditions will not change the landscape one iota. We as
a society are in a rut, and that is why we do such a poor
job of raising boys. At the same time, there is much value
in the traditions of our past, and it would be foolish to
jettison the whole without first thinking and feeling deeply
about the ways we need to modify our own assumptions.

How many times when talking to your children have you
heard words coming out of your mouth and been struck by
the thought that these are not really your words at all, but
they are a replay of words you heard from your parents,
words they probably heard from their parents, and so on
down the generations?

In this chapter I highlight some key places where we can
fall victim to our own training right when we want to blaze
a new trail for our sons. And this too is one of the great
gifts of parenting. In the process of teaching, nurturing,
and guiding, we grow.

Examine Gender Roles

> *"Men work hard, dole out punishment, do the yard work, and handle the cash. Women take care of the kids, do the cooking and housework, and take care of the hugs and kisses. Real old-fashioned, but that's what I learned growing up, and even though I don't agree with it anymore it is still pretty well ingrained."*

The past forty years have seen a tremendous shift in how we view gender roles, thanks largely to the millions of women who have demanded fuller and more equal participation in life. But don't fool yourself into thinking we have turned the corner. Cultural patterns of thousands of years aren't changed in a few decades; we are in the position of the battleship that has just turned the helm but will take another twenty miles before the ship actually makes its turn. In addition, the advances made by women have not been matched by men. Where women's lives have blossomed with opportunities, men's lives are for the most part still stuck in the old ways.

One way you can begin to have a real impact on your sons is to play down the gender role divisions in your own home. Start with how you divide up the chores and allocate responsibilities, and change the jobs you give your children. Examine the ways you are silently perpetuating old gender stereotypes. You might be comfortable with them, but by consciously breaking them up you send a powerful message to your children that their options have broadened considerably.

Parents: Include boys in dishwashing, cooking, or babysitting, and include girls in yard work, balancing the checkbook, and moving furniture around. It may seem like a small gesture, but it sends the message that all activities can be open to all of us.

Teachers: Create a lesson plan that focuses on the way gender and jobs have changed over the years. There is great material here. For example, did you know that in the early days of industrialization all secretaries and phone operators were men? Talk about both the huge influx and then departure from the workforce of women during and immediately after World War II. Collect data from your class about jobs held by mothers and fathers. Compare them to jobs held by grandmothers and grandfathers.

Know that Real Men Know How to Be Fathers

"When my two children were still very small, I became the full-time stay-at-home parent and my wife worked. It was the most incredibly rich and intense experience I have ever had, but it had its downside as well. I'd be sitting in the park with my kids surrounded by all these moms furtively stealing

glances at me and wondering what the hell was wrong with this guy."

Encouraging boys to remain connected to their emotions requires the full and active engagement of their fathers. Yet, too many fathers let this, the most valuable contribution they can make to their sons' development, slip away. Sometimes the hesitation is out of awkwardness and inexperience—we weren't raised to be nurturing parents, we weren't given even the basic information about caring for infants and toddlers, so the easy way is simply to back away and leave it to Mom. Sometimes the hesitation comes from outside pressure, social expectations, and, particularly, pressure from the workplace that gives the message: "If you want to get ahead, you must put your job ahead of your children."

But what father would actually endorse that message? Being a father today requires a very different kind of courage, the kind that anchors us to our deeper priorities, gives us the strength and commitment to pioneer for our sons a new and more fully integrated way of living. It means being mindful of the pressures that pull us away from our children. It means stepping firmly into the whirlwind of emotions that are part of growing up. It means adding our voices to the rising swell of women's voices demanding flexible work hours and corporate support rather than resistance to employees with families.

Parents: Fathers need to demonstrate through their words and actions that their children's emotional needs are just as high a priority as providing food and shelter. Reassess your work schedule and make sure it allows you to be with your children when they need you. Reassess the level and quality of your involvement at home and make sure that you are doing your share.

Teachers: Invite parents to bring several babies of different ages into your classroom. Allow the students to observe the babies' behavior. Help kids get comfortable with the care and nurturing of infants.

Men, Reacquaint Yourself with YOUR Feelings

"Being a father has been the single most important thing that has happened in my life. Not only because I love my kids so much, but because by being so actively involved in their lives, I have gotten the opportunity to go back and relearn through them a lot about acknowledging and respecting my own feelings."

For most men, the process of growing up is a process of growing further and further away from their emotions. We might characterize it more positively as "being under control," "being strong," or "being logical," but for many of us, our dispassionate calm has come at great cost. We have lost the ability to experience and to express our deepest feelings.

The good news is that being a father is the single best way to reconnect to our own emotions and relearn the skills necessary to integrate them fully into our lives. The reason is simple—our children are roiling bundles of emotions, and much of what they spend their childhood doing is trying to recognize, understand, and deal with these powerful feelings. If we take the opportunity they offer us by virtue of their unconditional love, if we engage ourselves earnestly in their lives, their concerns, their hopes and dreams, thoughts and feelings, we will not only reinforce for them the value and importance of this roller-coaster journey, but we will learn with them how to balance, integrate, and harness the power of our emotions.

Parents: Many new parents, even those strongly committed to sharing the childrearing, tend to find themselves in a routine where Mom is doing the lion's share of infant care. Don't let it happen! The sooner and more deeply Dad gets involved in the feeding, changing, dressing, cuddling, rocking, bathing, playing, and goo goo ga ga-ing, the better. For Dad, this is a once-in-a-lifetime opportunity that has the potential to change his life dramatically for the better.

Teachers: Express your own feelings about world events or subjects you are studying and invite your students to express theirs. Develop service projects, plays, or artwork that help students act on deep feelings and passions in positive ways.

Beware of Parental Imbalance

"After years of estrangement I've finally gotten to know my father, and what surprises me is that he is really a very tenderhearted guy. Growing up, my parents sort of divided up the parenting duties so that she was the carrot and Dad was the stick. It set up a 'just wait till your father gets home' pattern that pushed us further and further apart."

One of the most difficult things about parenting is trying to balance all the responsibilities in a way that won't allow our children to unconsciously put either Mom or Dad into a false and incomplete posture. This is easier said than done. With the pull of traditional roles still very much a factor, plus the practical divisions of labor necessitated by careers and time constraints and personality differences, it may seem easier to have Mom do the holding and reassuring and Dad lay down the law. But if we take the easy way out, we invite our sons to project their own distorted conclusions onto our accommodations—Mom is nice, loving, and supportive and Dad is the tough guy.

From that simple beginning can unfold an ingrained gender bias that robs everyone of what is real and essential—the full, amazing complexity of being human. If Dad is the sole instrument of punishment, then it is easy, almost natural, to take a few steps back and seek support when you need it from Mom, and to assume that men just can't be loving. If only Mom is the nurturing one, then maybe nurturing is exclusively women's work and not something that can be expected from men. And finally, in the face of this widening gulf, what am I supposed to be like when I become a man?

Parenting is hard work, and one of the hardest things we need to do is present our children with the full range of human capacity without artificially dividing it up into men's work and women's work. Both parents need to be nurturing and both need to be tough. We need our sons to see both their mother and their father artfully sharing and utilizing the full range of parental responsibilities.

Parents: Make a determined effort to share as equally as possible all parenting tasks, particularly the most tender emotional support and the most difficult parental disciplining.

Teachers: Students often comment that their favorite teachers are those who are both strict and kind, tough and fair. What can you do in your classroom to express both your caring and your expectation that they will live within the rules? How might you include them in creating a classroom climate that encourages them to be kind to one another, while reminding one another of class guidelines for safety and high standards in their work?

Make Special Father Time

"My dad was very much the old-school dad. He didn't talk too much and certainly not about anything that got close to being emotional, but somehow it never got in the way of making me feel special, because he went out of his way to spend time with me—even taking up tennis (he was pretty bad at it, too) just to have an excuse to be with me."

In a perfect world we would all—men, women, and children—be able to express our love and communicate the depths of our feelings, but we don't live in a perfect world. And for many fathers the words of love don't come easily. The more powerful the feelings, the more difficulty we seem to have finding words, and of course our feelings run very deep for our children. Unfortunately, our first reaction when faced with this uncomfortable position is to back away even further—to remove ourselves to a place that is less charged and more comfortable, and in doing so we drift away from our children.

We do it unconsciously, and we need to consciously change gears and try instead to find ways to bring us closer to our sons. One obvious way is to communicate directly, including writing notes or letters even if it seems forced. But we can always take advantage of the most precious commodity we have—our time. Traditionally, men in our society are judged by what they do, and as one-sided as this is, we can at the very least communicate indirectly by regularly and enthusiastically doing things with our sons— play with them, relax with them, engage them in activities or projects, be with them. Show them by the commitment of time that they are centrally important to us, and that it is with them that we wish to spend this time and share these moments.

Parents: Dad: Block out a good-sized piece of time just for the two of you on a regular basis and make it a priority—go fishing, take a hike. He'll remember the special times forever. Mom: If Dad is not on the scene, find a willing man—an uncle, a friend. Boys need alone time with a father figure.

Teachers: Plan a special time for dads or male friends to visit your classroom. Have a potluck, skating, or bowling party to which each student can bring a special older man.

Welcome Your Son's Tears

"I remember a time when I was very young and my sister and I got into a huge fight—a screaming, hitting, hair-pulling brawl that left both of us upset and in tears. My parents hugged and consoled my sister and sent me to my room without even asking what had happened. Thirty-something years later, it still hurts every time I think about it."

Boys shouldn't cry. This belief is so ingrained in our conditioning that it has become a cliché, and as a cliché we dismiss it casually—we know it isn't true. But we should not dismiss it, since in our dismissal we become sloppy, and in our sloppiness, we revert to the way we were conditioned. Without even knowing it, an eyebrow raises, our body language gives us away, an embarrassed "Stop crying, you're OK" comes out, and our small sons read it all too clearly—the disappointment, the judgment, the condemnation for expressing "inappropriate" emotions.

We need instead to see the tears of our boys as the great gifts they are, the opportunity to share and reinforce the importance of experiencing rather than avoiding pain and sadness. Such a simple statement may sound out of place in the midst of an "act happy at any cost—even if it means taking Prozac—culture," but each of us knows that sadness and pain are a normal part of life. We cannot eliminate them; we can only learn how to deal with them in a healthy manner. Yet, everything in our culture strips our young sons of any meaningful connection to their own sorrow; if we allow that process to take place, all that pain and sadness will simply reemerge as anger—generalized and justified anger at being treated as something less than a full person.

Parents: Set your internal alarm clock to go off every time you see tears or any signs of sadness from your son—not to shun or shame him but to engage him with as much empathy as you can muster. And don't be put off if he doesn't want to talk about it—it is not so important what he says, but it is crucially important what you say. Let him know that his feelings are natural, understandable, and an important reflection of who he is. Yes, help him learn how to deal with his sadness, but not until you first acknowledge the validity of his feelings.

Teachers: Tears, or any highly charge emotions, in the classroom can be very difficult to deal with, but at minimum, be on guard and prepared to deflect the derision that often emerges as group pressure to avoid the uncomfortable.

> If possible, turn the class discussion into an opportunity to
> understand. Invite students to talk about their sadness, perhaps
> at the death of a grandparent or pet.

Don't Tease

> *"Teasing was the male mode of communication in my family.
> With three brothers and my father, dinnertime was an
> exercise in seeing who could come up with the most clever
> insults and the wittiest comebacks. If you could strip away
> all the words and managed to decode the elaborate meaning
> underneath, there was love there, but over time the sheer
> weight of the words took their toll."*

Teasing is an art form for boys and men, a way for them,
usually unconsciously, to express their feelings. It comes
in three varieties: malicious, indifferent, and affectionate,
and each of them is damaging in its own way. Malicious
teasing is easy to spot and just as easy to object to. It can
be seen and understood for exactly what it is, a verbal
attack, and it should never be allowed to go unaddressed.

Indifferent teasing is the trash talk of playgrounds and
playing fields. It has worked its way so deeply into our
culture that we not only accept it but encourage it, even

though it demeans both the speaker and the object of the teasing. But far and away the most dangerous form of teasing is that which, ironically, is intended as a signal of affection.

For boys and men, trapped in the cultural straitjacket that defines a man, teasing is a crippled and heavily coded attempt to make their affectionate feelings known—we tease those we love, and the hidden message is that we wouldn't bother to tease them if we didn't love them. But the code is unspoken, and even if we know and accept the code, still the weight of the words wears the listener down. Teasing is sideways communication, and we owe it to our sons to help them learn to express their caring feelings directly.

Male teasing does the most damage when we tease our own children. It doesn't matter if "it is only teasing"; it doesn't matter if it is in fact our way of saying, "I love you." The children are young; they do not know the intricate unspoken code of teasing; and even if they can sense that something else exists under these words, the words themselves bite and sting, particularly when encoded within the tease is a fragment of real criticism. When we model teasing, our children are likely to fall into this secondhand communication style.

Parents: Express your love, appreciation, and admiration directly, and encourage your boys to do so, too.

Teachers: Be aware of the ways you may fall into teasing your students. Sarcasm can eat away at your relationships with them quickly. Talk with them about the effects of teasing. Make a communication lesson out of discovering more positive and direct ways to get a message across.

Avoid Shaming

> *"I think I was fifteen at the time. My parents had been out of town for two days and I was on my own. They got back three hours early and the kitchen—which I had delayed cleaning till the last moment—was still a mess. My father just looked at me with this withering expression of disappointment. Suddenly all my excuses and explanations just got caught in my throat."*

Our boys are under constant and enormous pressure to act like some idealized image of a man. They are taught they must be strong, mature, accomplished, and responsible, and must not make mistakes. That is a crushingly unfair burden to place on a small boy or a young man, and the emotional coup de grâce occurs when we shame them with words, looks, or silence when they inevitably fail.

The deliverance of a message of shame, almost automatically the response when our boys fail to live up to our expectations, does more damage in an instant than is imaginable. It reinforces the distorted and unattainable cultural image of perfection, and tells them in painful measure that until they succeed in becoming this illusion, they have failed in our eyes. It has this devastating effect even if we think we have only been disappointed in a small way, since they cannot read our minds and all they see, hear, and feel is our disappointment.

By choosing shame over discussion we sever our connection to them, as if it were too painful to remain connected to one who could fail so miserably. Everything is heightened, and all we accomplish is the brutal dismantling of their already shaky sense of self-worth and the removal of any healthy avenue for understanding and empathy.

Parents: Words and actions that shame our sons are among the most damaging mistakes we can make as parents. We all falter, we all do things and say things that fall short of even our own expectations. Our boys, caught up in the incredibly difficult endeavor of trying to grow into men, will falter and fail time and time again. That is when they need us to be there, with love, with understanding, with words that deepen our connection to them. Avoid shaming behavior at all costs.

Teachers: Transform situations when your students really "blew it" from times filled with shame into opportunities for learning. Discuss what thinking and behavior went into the mistake. Explore possible options to try in similar situations.

Watch the Double Standard in Discipline

> *"My parents were the masters of the double standard. Being a boy, I was allowed to do things my sister wasn't, and boy did she resent that. What she of course never noticed was the other side of the coin. When she did something wrong, she was allowed to vent, cry, complain, and blame everything and everyone else. When I screwed up the hammer came down fast and furious, no if's, and's, or but's."*

Do you have different standards for girls' and boys' behavior? Do you give more slack to your daughter because you assume she will not get into as much trouble? Do you allow her to yell back at you, but clamp down if your son says one word?

We unconsciously reinforce the message that our boys' feelings are not important in the way we discipline them. We tend to be very firm and unrelenting, as if we are afraid that showing any compassion will be a sign of weakness that they will instantly exploit. We tend to be more afraid of boys turning "bad" than we are of girls doing so, and our fear may cause us to overreact. Also, we are used to girls expressing emotions and are more comfortable with their venting than we are with boys.

Ironically, out of our desire to provide strong guidance and enforce strong boundaries, we act from a place of weakness—we present boys with a tough, disappointed, even angry face and solemnly announce their punishment with no appeal allowed. In so doing we have denied them the opportunity to experience the full range of emotions that might normally accompany such a situation and have sent them off to stew in isolation.

It doesn't matter that many of the emotions they might want to express are off the mark or even inappropriate. If they never get a chance to air those feelings and examine them in a supportive context, how will they ever learn the significance of the feeling itself, the importance of understanding where it came from, and its relevance to the situation? Trying to raise our boys to be more aware of their feelings means opening the door all the way, perhaps most important, to sharing feelings that are off the mark.

Parents: Notice if you behave differently when disciplining your daughter and son. Begin to see discipline as the opportunity it

truly is, an emotionally charged moment where you can help
the boy in your life come to grips with even his wildest feelings.

Teachers: Examine your discipline practices. Are you more
likely to give girls the benefit of the doubt? Do you let boys
off the hook more often? Consider establishing a grievance
process that allows both boys and girls the chance to express
verbally or visually their feelings about the rules and any
incidents they are involved in.

Check Out Your Gender Fears

*"I was the only boy in a family with four sisters. I was
also the youngest, and my sisters used to dress me up for
'productions' they wanted to put on. One day my father came
home early and saw me all dressed up like a beauty queen
and he blew a fuse."*

We all have gender boundaries, and when those are
crossed, we get uncomfortable. Beneath most of them,
especially those concerning boys, is an often-unconscious
fear of homosexuality. After all, where did the notion
of the "sissy" come from except from the fear that a boy
might be gay?

If we don't examine our fears around this complex issue,
we might be squashing our son's emotional sensitivity out

of a misguided attempt to "keep" our sons from becoming gay. (Most research supports the belief that homosexuality is a genetic trait, just as heterosexuality is, and that sexual preference is generally born, not made.) I once knew a woman who was so afraid of her son being gay that she became extremely anxious and ridiculed him for wanting to cook, to sew, and to play music. He's an adult now, and despite his desire to do such "feminine" things, is a happily married heterosexual with a beautiful daughter.

When we exhibit anxiety over our boys being "too" feminine, we teach them there is something wrong with being nurturing and sensitive and reinforce their need to be macho to be a man. And if our son is gay, we send him terribly destructive messages that we don't love him as he is.

Parents: Think for a minute about what is, to you, acceptable and unacceptable behavior for boys: Crying? Playing with dolls? Hugging a male friend over the age of five? The more we come to know how *we* feel, the less we will react unconsciously.

Teachers: Notice how you perceive gender roles in your classroom. Are there jobs you give only to girls and not to boys? Consider offering all options to everyone and notice what new skills boys and girls alike might learn. Allow students to question their own assumptions and broaden their experience of "appropriate" behavior.

Discover the Source of His Wildness

> *"The first five years I was in school were one long drawn-out battlefield between me, my parents, and my teachers. I was constantly in the principal's office, suspended a bunch of times, and had the reputation as the top troublemaker at the school. My parents use to try to defend me by telling my teachers I was just a 'high-spirited' little boy."*

Every culture tries to gloss over the consequences of its mistakes by coming up with homilies that excuse but don't explain. One of the most damaging excuses we have developed to explain away our boys' inappropriate behavior is simply that "boys will be boys." "Of course, he's a little wild, he's got so much energy because he's a boy!" Once the excuses fall flat and the inappropriate behavior continues, we diagnose them with Attention Deficit Disorder (ADD) or some other sophisticated-sounding conclusion and put them on drugs. Recent studies have documented an explosion of ADD diagnoses, and not surprisingly the proportion of boys as compared to girls put on medication is literally off the charts.

But could so many boys have ADD? Or is much of the inappropriate behavior of boys simply a cry for help from small, scared children set adrift in an emotional world where they don't have either the resources or the support to understand or control what is going on?

We need to begin to see behavior problems for what they are—desperate cries for help. If we were standing on our front steps and heard our son calling for help, our hearts would start to race, and we would rush immediately to his aid. We can do nothing less when his cry for help comes in the guise of misbehavior. We need to act as quickly as possible to try to get to the bottom of what is really going on, to discover the underlying emotional issues that are eliciting this alarm.

Parents: See behavior problems for what they are and intervene immediately. Are boundaries or limits not being properly and consistently set? Are your son's emotions hidden and unaddressed? Is he acting out because he doesn't know how to speak out? Boys aren't de facto genetically out of control, and it is our responsibility to find the source even if it requires professional help.

Teachers: This is a difficult and challenging area for teachers, who bear much of the brunt of behavior problems. Drugging boys may be the easiest solution, but is it the best in the long run? If you understand something of the source of the problem, try to provide what is missing as much as possible, be it encouragement, support, or simply strong and consistent boundaries. Raise the issue with parents in a compassionate manner, emphasizing how important the issue is to their son's development. Investigate the possibility that a child's misbehavior reflects an important learning need—to be more physically or verbally involved, for example.

Avoid Labels

> *"In my family, I was 'the klutz,' my younger sister was 'the crybaby,' my older sister was 'the smart one,' and my older brother was 'headstrong.' It's amazing to me how hard we all tried to live up to our names."*

Labels are incredibly useful. The ability to categorize and assign labels is one of the hallmarks of human consciousness that allows us to process and access vast amounts of information with ease. But when raising children, labels should be avoided at all costs. When we use labels with our children, even "good" labels, we bring into being a powerful set of expectations that our children may not be able or may not want to live up to but will never be able to escape. We not only unconsciously create pressures on them to act in a way that we have (usually) very casually decreed, but we also shut them off from a whole other range of possibilities.

The very powerful if unarticulated message we send is that you are supposed to be like *this* (uncoordinated, headstrong, brilliant, funny, sweet, well-behaved, strong) with the equally unstated threat that if you fail to live up to my label there is something wrong with you. Not only do labels restrict and direct the supposedly "acceptable" channels for our children's growth, but at the same time they send the damaging message that our children are supposed to pay attention to what other people think about them and try to be what other people want them to be.

Parents: Avoid labeling your children. If your son has strong characteristics, it's fine to talk about them, but not in a way that makes the child feel the characteristic defines who he is. For example, "I see you feel strongly about this," rather than, "You are always so stubborn!"

Teachers: Labels can be limiting in the classroom. Create an ongoing dialogue with your students about their many gifts and challenges. In speaking with them, use specific phrases that describe behavior, rather than "character" labels—"Your writing here is full of action and feeling," rather than "You're a good writer." Help them know the specific skills they are developing well and specific ways to take their learning further.

Talk Straight about Tough Subjects

"There were so many topics that couldn't be raised in my family that by the time I was ready to leave the nest, we were pretty much reduced to rehashing the same old themes over and over again."

One of the things that surprised me when doing the research for my earlier book *Fathering* was that almost all of the fathers I interviewed had never spoken to another man about the issues they struggled with as a father. Can you imagine finding even a single mother who hasn't had at least a hundred such conversations with her friends? The difference is tragic, and it derives from how we raise our boys and how we raise our girls. Girls are encouraged to talk—to question, to wonder, to express their confusion, to not know the answers, and to seek help from others. Boys are raised to at least pretend they know the answers, and if they don't, to at least not admit it by asking for help. The comical manifestation of this phenomenon is the old joke about men never asking for directions.

We need to counter this tendency by talking to our boys about tough issues, like pornography and masturbation, that are uncomfortable; the ones like spirituality and values, where answers are very personal; the ones like politics and philosophy, where we often degenerate into arguments instead of open-ended dialogue. When we pull away from these subjects, we send our boys back into their own isolated worlds.

We cut them off and offer them no avenue of assistance, guidance, or comfort, and we simply reinforce the foolish notion that somehow they will automatically become men who have all the answers. When we encourage our boys to seek out help with difficult matters, we help them become men who will reach out when they need to.

Parents: Engage your boys in real dialogue about anything and everything that is important. Pay close attention to the issues you feel yourself shying away from. Imagine, if it causes you this much distress to think about and talk about, just how difficult it must be for your young son.

Teachers: Allow time for both small and large group discussions about issues of importance to your students. Invite them to generate a list of topics, both deep and frivolous. Listening and speaking skills can be developed with any topic.

Encourage Interdependence

"We were pretty poor when I was a kid, but I think one of the best things about it was that it forced us to rely on aunts, uncles, grandparents, and even cousins a lot more than most of my friends. I grew up in a large, somewhat dysfunctional, but ultimately very loving group of people, and I think it has served me very well."

A much observed but little studied phenomenon of the past fifty years is how common it has become for boys to grow up into men and then drift further and further away from their families. We know it happens, we make excuses for it happening—"Oh, he is so busy now with his new job and the new baby on the way." But we never address the real damage done by what has become a national tragedy.

Emotional distance is not encoded in the male genes; it is a sad result of our own behavior.

Boys drift away from their families because unconsciously we raise them to do exactly that. We start pushing them into independence at an early age; send them mixed signals about what we want and need from them, so that they are almost certain to fail us; spend little time or energy building strong family ties; and then wonder why they flee to a safe distance.

If we want our sons to remain close to us, we need to hold them warmly and lovingly within the larger embrace of the family. They need to feel like they belong; they need to feel and experience the love, nonjudgmental interest and respect of their parents, grandparents, and as many aunts, uncles, and cousins as can fit. These are ties with history and deep roots; they do not disappear easily, but we need to nourish them, and that means taking the time to do things together, spending the energy to incorporate them into the heart of the larger family. The payoff for everyone is incalculable; the sadness if we fail is equally incalculable.

We need to teach our sons not just independence, but interdependence: that none of us can manage alone, and that we are all stronger for relying on one another.

Parents: Some families are born; others are made. If you do not have an extended family, make one! Find honorary grandparents, aunts, uncles, and cousins. Teach your son that loving connections are one of his strongest assets in life, and model staying connected to those you care about.

Teachers: Help kids become aware of who they can turn to and rely on beyond their immediate families. Invite them to choose six people in their lives who are older than they are. Have them brainstorm about each person's skills and abilities. Then have them write letters, conduct meetings, or make phone calls to learn more about each of the six.

Understand the Complexities of Adolescence

"My teenage years were just pure hell."

Adolescence can be the most difficult time in a boy's life, and there are many factors contributing to the challenge. With the onset of puberty, a whole new set of sensations are surging through his body and jumbling up many of the thoughts and feelings he has grown used to. It is also a time when he starts to feel an urgency about "growing up," believing that somehow he is supposed to have magically figured everything out, including knowing who he is and what he wants to do in his life. Yet even under the best of circumstances our adolescent boys lack many of the resources and the necessary years of experience to even begin to feel comfortable about these larger life issues.

On top of all that, popular culture sends a wildly distorted image that proclaims that these years are really the "wonder years," the best time of your life. The cumulative effect can put enormous pressure on our boys. During this time, they desperately need us to be there for them, supporting them, reminding them that it is sheer folly to expect to have answers to questions many *adults* are still struggling with, and providing them the strong current of love they need just to stumble their way through. And yet, at precisely this moment of need, far too many parents back away. Either out of a misguided sense that "they need to sort this out on their own," or sometimes because we don't have a clue what to do with this gawky flailing creature.

The research is clear: The more parents are actively engaged in their adolescent boy's life the less trouble he gets into, the less involvement in drugs, gangs, and antisocial activities, and the better his grades and the higher his self-esteem. This is a crucial time in their lives, and we must be up to the challenge.

Parents: As your sons grow into their teenage years, escalate your engagement in their lives. This is the time they need you more than they ever will again. Read *Wonderful Ways to Love a Teen* by Judy Ford. If you find this time of your son's life particularly challenging, consider joining a support group.

Teachers: An open door policy, even for specific hours each week, can signal to your students that you are willing to engage beyond the classroom. Sponsor a club in an area of your personal interest. Your involvement in their lives beyond the class is crucial to boys this age.

CHAPTER 3

Developing New Attitudes and Behaviors

Since most of us were raised under the "old rules" that defined what a man was supposed to be, merely examining our outdated assumptions is not enough. Raising our sons with high emotional intelligence is an extraordinary opportunity to grow beyond our own training and become the more balanced and integrated people we want to see mirrored in our sons.

For many of us, particularly men, that means learning new behaviors: learning how to open our own hearts, to communicate our love in ways that he will feel it, to live our own lives deeply as an example for our sons, to own up to our mistakes and apologize, and to nurture our own emotional intelligence so that we can be even more finely attuned to the emotional needs of our sons.

Tell Him You Love Him

> *"I don't remember my father ever telling me he loved me. It bothered me so much that when I had children, I decided I was going to tell them I loved them all the time. My son is now in his twenties, and when I tell him I love him, he is always a wee bit embarrassed, but I can still tell that he loves hearing it."*

I doubt that anyone has ever tried to study how often girls as opposed to boys are told they are loved by their parents, but I would place a very large bet on the results. How did this particularly bad habit slip into our behavior? Boys need to know they are loved just as much as girls, and at times even more than girls simply because they can so easily drift away from the warm embrace of that love.

They need that reassurance on a regular basis, and for the most part we don't do a good job of providing it.

It certainly isn't because we don't love them! I have never spoken to a parent who didn't love his or her son deeply, but all the cultural debris surrounding how boys should be treated has pushed us into this tragically awkward place where we are afraid to say something as true and important as "I love you." And they squirm every time they hear it.

But words are powerful, especially when they fill that squirmy place, and the absence of those words creates an ever-widening void of emptiness between you and the boy in your life. Love isn't something we can assume, and it isn't something we can presume is understood. Love is the foundation that is absolutely essential for any relationship, and it makes no sense at all to leave it out of our regular vocabulary.

Parents: Make a commitment to tell your son you love him every day. Do it with feeling and don't be put off because sometimes it feels awkward. It is true, it is necessary, and it needs to be articulated. Don't just presume he "knows."

Teachers: Find comfortable and appropriate ways to express your affection and appreciation. "I think you're terrific" is just as important for our boys to hear in school as "I love you" is at home.

Realize He Needs Dad's Help

"When I was growing up, I was always looking at my father trying to figure out the secret of what a man was supposed to be, and sometimes it seemed to me that he was almost purposefully hiding all the answers I needed."

Most of us who are fathers today don't know what we are doing. We even joke about it: "He didn't come with an owner's manual!" It is a testament to how woefully inept we have been as a culture that we arrive at the single most important job we will ever do in our lives completely and totally unprepared. In any other situation, we would be quite properly fired immediately and shown the door.

Being a father today is uniquely challenging because it is our task to redefine the meaning of what it is to be a man and a father. We are supposed to do this with little or no training in the world of emotions, and little or no support. We also have no choice if we want to give our own sons the best chance of growing into strong, well-rounded, and emotionally integrated men.

But where do we start? What are we supposed to do? In all the interviews I have conducted with men, one of the biggest obstacles I see is our own fear of what we don't know. Many of us are so uncertain we simply grind to a halt and do nothing. It's like trying to learn a complicated dance step and getting stuck on the second move. The feelings are there, but they are a swirling jumble without a clear outlet.

I've learned the best way to fumble through is simply to fumble through—admit you aren't sure of what to say or what needs to be done, admit that this is new territory but too important to remain unexplored. Then say or do what seems the best under the circumstances. You are his father, and, as long as you are as honest as you can be and try as hard as you can to help him sort this world out, you will always be his hero.

Parents: Dads, talk to your sons about emotions. Yes, it's hard, but if you don't, the message becomes clear that this is not a subject men talk about. Share your own difficulties in this area, help him to understand the consequences of growing up without access to or a deep understanding of his own emotional world. Moms, be as supportive as you possibly can and remember that this may sometimes mean backing away and giving Dad room to do this his way.

Teachers: When class lessons lead to an appropriate exploration of the emotions behind or generated by the events under discussion, have students imagine what they would have felt in those circumstances. Be particularly careful to bring the boys into the discussion in a supportive way.

Take Turns When Necessary

"One of the things I really appreciate about my parents is that I never got the silent treatment. There was always a doorway back into their good graces. If I had a heated argument with my dad, Mom would show up in my room to talk. If Mom and I were at odds, Dad would suddenly appear to talk it through.

That was a security blanket for me, knowing that even if I screwed up, they'd find a way to get us all back together."

Nobody ever said parenting was easy, particularly if you are trying to do it differently than it was done to you. There are times when you are at your wit's end, and all you want to do is say things that are not at all constructive in a tone of voice that will only make matters worse. That's the time to pass the baton. By definition, raising a son in a manner that allows him to experience and learn to deal with his full range of emotions is going to lead to some emotionally charged situations. He isn't going to become an expert overnight in expressing his frustration, disappointment, sadness, or anger in calm and perfectly appropriate ways, and no matter how much we try, we aren't always going to be able to artfully bend and respond.

When you feel your own temperature rising and know that you are operating below the level of calm maturity you'd like to bring to any engagement with your son, take a big step back and let someone else enter as the intermediary. Particularly after a heated argument, this can bring a calm "neutral" into the mix, giving both you and your son the opportunity to calm down and reexamine the real issues. It can help you more gracefully spot those times when assumptions or behavior have contributed significantly to the disconnection.

Then, when you have both calmed down and gotten more clarity about what the issues are, you can go back and try to find a resolution that will bring you closer together rather than pushing you further apart.

Parents: This is easier to do if both of you live in the same house, but even in a divorce situation, you can take turns being the sounding board, as long as you don't demonize the other parent: "Oh yes, he's so terrible—that's why I left him." If you can't do this for your ex-spouse in a healthy way, perhaps your mother or father, an aunt or uncle, or a family friend can assume this role. It is vital that we all have help from a neutral, reasonable adult.

Teachers: We all don't relate equally well to all students. With kids that push your buttons, find colleagues who relate well with them and talk about these kids together. Play mediator for each other when things heat up. Help each other discover what you need when you reach your limit rather than taking your feelings out on the student.

Notice the Enemy in the Living Room

"My parents joke all the time about how I was raised by the television. Now that I have my own children, that joke isn't so funny anymore."

The easiest dangers to ignore are those that have worked their way so deeply into our lives that we no longer see them as dangers. So take a few hours and watch some television. Forget for a moment that you are an adult who can distinguish between right and wrong, and watch television as if you were an alien trying to discover what makes humans tick. I guarantee it will be a sobering experience, made all the more so when you realize that that is how our children perceive television, and that television is a most pervasive influence on them.

Who's really raising *your* son? Recent studies reveal that the time children spend watching television is fifty-six times greater than the time they spend with their fathers and eleven times greater than the time spent with their mothers! Then think for a moment about the escalating incidents of violence on television—somewhere around thirty-plus violent acts per television hour. If we are to raise a new generation of boys who have the values, resources, and emotional maturity that we want them to have, we can't simply ignore the enemy in the living room just because it can sometimes be a friend.

Parents: Take control. Watch only shows that model positive human values. Rigorously restrict access to the television— don't fall into the trap of using the tube as a babysitter! When you do watch television, talk about what you are watching.

Teachers: Deconstruct a popular television show and get the children involved in posing and answering deeper questions about what kind of values and behaviors the show is modeling. Teach children how to watch television with a critical eye.

Be Yourself

"Sometimes when I'm dealing with my son, I get so wound up in trying to figure out what I should say, how I should approach him, how I should react, that I become so stiff and unnatural that even I can't stand to listen to myself."

Just as our boys get lost sometimes, we too get lost—being a parent is not easy, and it's not like we got a whole lot of training in doing it right. Most of us are just trying to fumble along as best we can, relying on our deep love for our children and whatever insights we can pick up along the way. Yes, there are things we should know and think about, there are things we should do and things we should not do and attitudes we need to develop or reform, and all that can at times add up to brainlock. It's like a new golfer trying to remember the hundreds of little things that make up a good swing and butchering the ball in the process.

The best advice I can share is to relax and just be yourself. It won't be perfect, but at least it will be real, and that sense of real connection is the most precious link we have with our children. What they want and need from us is good honest presence and engagement in their lives. If you feel lost or confused, say so. And if you are feeling out-of-control angry, take some time by yourself before you reengage.

Parents: Don't get too caught up trying to be the perfect parent. You can't be. You can only be the best of *yourself*, and your son needs that much more than an encyclopedia of good parenting skills.

Teachers: Good teaching skills are a central requirement of your job, but don't let them squeeze your personality out of the classroom. Let your students see the real you; it will help imprint upon them the importance of being true to themselves.

Beware of Criticism!

"My dad was always correcting me. Even when I did something good, all he could see was what I could have done better. By the time I left for college, he and I were hardly

speaking. That bothered me so much I wrote him this really long letter trying to explain how I felt. I got it back with all my grammar and punctuation mistakes all marked up in red ink."

As parents, and particularly as fathers, we often can be overly critical of our sons. It is as if our own unspoken fear of how they will do in the world emerges, making us push them to do better and challenge them to try harder. There is nothing wrong with a good and appropriately timed challenge, but when it gets out of balance, our sons experience it as a constant reminder of their inadequacy instead of a loving nudge to do better. And when that happens, we have put ourselves out of reach, in a position where we can no longer be trusted with his real thoughts and feelings; because in his mind, our automatic response would be critical.

The most important job we face as parents of boys is always to stay strongly connected, no matter what it takes and no matter how difficult it is. If that means finding better ways to deal with our own fears about his future, or finding ways to provide insight and guidance without shutting down the deeper channels of communication, then that is our task. We can't simply stand back and say, "What's the matter with him, he never listens," because it is our job to treat him with the love and respect that assures that he will listen.

Parents: Be very careful about how, when, and why you criticize your son. Your intentions may be perfect, but this is very dangerous territory. Whenever you detect even the slightest pulling away or shutting down on the part of your son, drop everything else, even if the "issue" at hand seems important, and do whatever you need to do to first reestablish a strong trusting bond.

Teachers: Focus your interactions on what your students are doing well in both academics and behavior. Encourage them to evaluate their own performance before you do. Tell them specifically what you are looking for to keep criticism at a level that they can handle and learn from.

Don't Stop Hugging

"Once when my son was six, he and I were shopping at the supermarket. I don't remember what we were talking about, but we were having fun, clowning around, and at one point I picked him up and gave him a big hug. An elderly woman walking by stared at me in anger and said, 'You should be ashamed of yourself touching him like that.' I was so completely flabbergasted I couldn't even reply."

Who came up with the concept that boys hit a certain age and suddenly don't need to be hugged? It probably traces from a mixture of misinformed fears, including the fear of "turning" little boys into homosexuals, or in the category of more sophisticated mistakes, the fear of doing psychological damage by "impeding" his individuation process. Whatever the source, it is high time for it to be put to rest.

Good old-fashioned hugging and caring physical touch are some of the most potent magic elixirs that we possess. We all want and need to be touched, to be held, to be stroked. It is one of the most powerful and undeniable ways to give and receive real warmth and love, and it helps us to feel on a very visceral level that we are indeed deeply connected to the ones we love.

Withholding that incredible gift for any reason can be devastating, because no matter what we say about loving our son, it sends a message to him that he is now literally and figuratively isolated, outside the deeper circle of our love and caring. In our efforts to raise our sons to be more emotionally grounded, to have a better understanding and full access to their emotions, we need to do everything possible to keep them connected to us so they can feel and share the deepest aspects of our love.

Parents: Hug your boys and don't ever stop. Because of the cultural legacy that surrounds them, there will be times when they might resist, pull away, or feel embarrassed. Understand

and respect their feelings, but don't let it stop you from maintaining a regular caring physical bond.

Teachers: Whenever possible, make simple physical contact with your students—a touch on the arm, a pat on the back. With the fear of accusations and lawsuits, we are in danger of erasing important body language signals of support from our relationship vocabulary. Maintain your right to make clean, casual contact. It enhances learning for most students.

Praise Him

"One year I lost the final match in a tennis tournament to a kid I knew pretty well who had never beaten me. I was really upset with myself because I had played terribly. On the way home, my dad told me that he was really proud of how graciously I had congratulated the winner. I of course had been so caught up in my own feelings I could hardly remember doing it, but hearing Dad say that made me feel great, like I had really accomplished something after all."

From practically the moment they start walking, boys are the target of so much criticism, correcting, and complaining, it can seem to them that parents don't exist for any other purpose. That's why we have to try very hard to even out our instinct to pull our sons back into line with as much real praise as possible. And note the qualifier—it has to be real. Praising your son for playing a great game when he in fact played poorly will not only fall on deaf ears, it will put you in the category of those whose words can't be trusted.

But genuine praise is crucial because he needs to know that you are not only engaged enough in his life to see the things he is struggling with and the accomplishments that he is making, but that you are celebrating and affirming him every step of the way.

Be lavish with the kinds of things you praise him for as well. Don't restrict praise just to his sports or academic accomplishments. Those are fine, but navigating the difficult territory of growing up is much more challenging than baseball or midterms, and it is in this area—the thinking, feeling, and doing of character development—that he needs your support the most.

Parents: Praise him for his honesty—even when it arises by his admitting he did something wrong. Praise him for his generosity, his kindness, his consideration for others. Praise him for worrying about what is right and wrong, for recycling bottles and cans. Praise him for all the things he does and says that make you proud to be his parent.

Teachers: Real and specific praise is important in every learner's life. Have kids think, talk, and write about things people have said to them that have made them want to learn more or get more involved.

Grow Your Praise

> "I started playing soccer when I was seven, and whenever my dad watched he always patted me on the back and said, 'Good game, son.' In my senior year in high school, when I was being recruited by a number of pretty big soccer universities, it was still, 'Good game, son.'"

Routine can squeeze the meaning out of just about anything, even praise. Just getting done what needs to get done in raising children requires setting up routines, but it is easy to take this too far. If your son is a good writer and you have diligently praised his writing for years, the message "That's great" may have lost its impact years ago. The same goes for any area of his life: "You played a great game," or "That was very generous of you." All good in and of themselves, but they become meaningless with repetition.

As our boys become more proficient at life skills and develop aspects of their characters in deeper and more complex ways, we have to strive to show them that we notice their growth and are delighted by it: "I love the richness of the words you used to describe this," or "Your fielding seems to be much smoother and more natural now," or "I'm impressed that you were able to see your sister needed some support from you."

By growing our praise as they grow, we can help them feel appreciated and acknowledged in their accomplishments and show that we are deeply engaged with them on this beautiful journey of development.

Parents: Pay attention to the changes in your boy's development and let him know you both see and take joy in his growth. Look for new things to compliment and new ways to do it.

Teachers: It's easy to fall into using the same routine phrases in commenting on work. Remember, your specific, sincere comments can enhance learning and help each child feel known and supported.

Don't Be Afraid of a Strong Mother-Son Bond

"Sometime around eight or nine my mother passed me off to my father. That sounds weird saying it, but that was what it felt like. All of a sudden, I'd be trying to talk to her or do

> *something with her and she'd say, 'Go talk to your father,' or, 'Wait until your father gets home.' I never quite understood it, but I think it had something to do with me learning how to be a man."*

It is a longstanding myth in our culture that some time before adolescence boys need to "separate" from their mothers and identify with their fathers to grow up to be healthy men. Nothing could be further from the truth. To grow up with a broad integrated perspective on the world, we need all the gifts we can get—from our mothers, our fathers, our grandmothers and grandfathers, our adult friends, teachers, mentors, and anyone else who has the interest and energy to be a part of our growing up.

Artificially cutting off one source, particularly one so centrally important as our mothers, can be downright crippling. Traditionally, mothers have been the main reservoir of nurturance for boys, and arbitrarily walling that off on the basis of some moth-eaten mythology can push our sons outside the world of emotions altogether. That is exactly what we don't want to do.

This doesn't mean mothers are more important than fathers to a boy's development, but they are certainly equally as important as fathers. Our sons need both parents to offer as much of themselves as possible to the boys' world of experience, so that they will have the broadest and richest of resources from which to pick and choose the characteristics, values, thoughts, and ideals that will serve them best.

> **Parents:** Support a good healthy mother-son relationship in any way possible. Maybe Mom can take him to a baseball game or schedule regular time alone together.
>
> **Teachers:** Have your students consider what traits and important teachings they have gotten from their mothers. Create a celebration that honors the mother-child bond. Study the roles mothers have played in history.

Think Individuation, Not Separation

> *"One of the family stories my mom loves to tell was my first day at daycare. I think I was four, and apparently, I attached myself to her leg, started to howl, and wouldn't let go. It took three people to unwrap me and take me kicking and screaming into the center."*

As I discussed in the previous suggestion, one of the myths we have grown up with is that little boys have to be "encouraged" (as in forced) to separate from their mothers; otherwise they will grow up as weak-willed mama's boys.

Just about everything is wrong with this story. The first false aspect is that it isn't their mother they are trying to cling to, it's the person who has held them close in the warm full embrace of their heart. It could just as well have been their father. Of course, in our culture early childcare has been almost exclusively a mother's task (though fortunately, that is changing), so the mistake is perhaps easy to understand. The point is that we aren't talking about gender here; we are talking about little boys not wanting to give up the deep emotional connection they grew up with.

This is something we need to encourage, not discourage. We need to stop thinking in terms of forced separation and start thinking in terms of reinforcing our emotional bonds with our sons while at the same time encouraging them to wander out into the world and try out their wings—knowing that we will always be there for them. We want our sons to know that we will always hold the door to our hearts and arms open to them and that this close emotional bond will never go away.

Instead of separation from our sons, we need to begin to think in terms of individuation. The difference is profound. With separation, we say, "You need to go off now to become your own person." With individuation we say, "We want to support you in becoming who you were meant to be, and we will do whatever we can to help in that process because no one can make it on his or her own." Yes, there may be times when we need to nudge them a little, but we need to make sure they always know the connection will never be broken.

Parents: When your son begins exploring his own world, encourage him, support him, nudge him gently, but don't force him. Make sure he—and you—understand he can individuate without separating. And take special care to find ways to welcome him back that will communicate strongly the lasting and continual bond between you.

Teachers: Study stories with the themes of individuation and separation, "growing up" stories such as *Peter Pan* or *Little Man Tate.* Discuss the different views of what it means to be independent *and* connected. Have the kids write their own, "When I Grow Up..."

Check In Regularly

"I had a safety net when I was growing up. Sometimes I'd sink into a funk and it would feel like I couldn't find the door out. My mom would always notice and find exactly the right moment to slip in and ask me how I was feeling."

In a perfect world, we would all take responsibility for how we feel and what we think about what is happening to us, and part of that responsibility would be regularly reporting back to the ones we love. We don't live in a perfect world, and for our boys, who are struggling with a host of issues they can barely get their minds around, regular and open communication is sometimes not even on their radar screens.

Being a boy, particularly during the tumultuous teenage years, sometimes feels like constant information overload. Your hormones are triggering weird sensations that you have no experience with. Your brain is trying to process schoolwork, parental instructions, and social expectations—not to mention relationships with girls and worrying about where to apply to college. Your emotions are bouncing off the sides of your heart, and you are still too young and too inexperienced to know how to process all that is happening.

That's why we need to have our antennae up and be ready to dive in. But it has to done delicately, at the right moment and with the right attitude. The proper moment can be anytime, but the key is trying to find a quiet time and place without distractions so the compassion in your inquiry can be received. Just a simple heartfelt "How are you feeling," or "You seem upset (or bothered, or preoccupied). Is there anything I can do to help?" can do the trick, although there are times during the teenage years that any caring remark will be met with a snarl or a sneer. If that happens, back off and try again later.

The check-in needs to come from a place of real concern, and at the same time we must be willing to respect the silence if he isn't ready to talk.

Sometimes he will open up, sometimes he won't. But just the knowledge that we are going to be there, regularly checking in, will give him the security to know that he isn't alone with his swirling emotions.

Parents: Make checking in with your son a regular part of your life. If you don't live with your son, find a way—email, phone, whatever—to keep the line open. Even if you go for weeks and months without cracking the door to his heart open, keep at it.

Teachers: Sometimes kids in turmoil will open up more readily to someone they trust who is not their parent. Check in with your students casually on a regular basis. Stay alert to changes in a child's demeanor that might be a call for help.

Dads: 'Fess Up!

"Sometimes I feel like a total fraud. I'm sitting on my son's bed laying down the rules or giving him advice like I actually know what I'm doing, and the truth is, I'm as unsure of a lot

> *of the very same issues he's concerned about as he is, and the only advantages I have are a couple decades of experience and a more polished ability to reason."*

Virtually every man who grew up in this culture still holds on to a bit of the male myth that when we grow up, we'll be calm, strong, problem-solvers and have all the answers readily at hand. If we are willing to admit it, we even get to experience that feeling when our children are very little, and that is exactly how they see us.

It's a great feeling until we realize that our poor children are being completely deluded and we are just struggling to do the best we can. So one thing we really need to do is resist the impulse to pretend we have all the answers.

That in itself would be a great gift to our sons. As long as we try to maintain the illusion of penetrating and all-encompassing wisdom, our sons will be overwhelmed with the thought that they too are supposed to become so wise—only they also know for certain they will never get there. By upholding an image of perfection, we completely undermine their confidence and reinforce an unrealistic fantasy image of what a man should be.

To go one step further, when your son faces a difficult situation or problem, take every opportunity you can to admit your own struggles in dealing with these issues.

Tell stories of stupid things you did or said, or of times you were deeply hurt or affected by what others said or did. Become not only fallible in his eyes, but a source of strength, so that he can see that confusion in this territory is par for the course, and by the way, Dad is someone he can talk to about this.

Parents: Dads: As fathers we need to shed our mantle of all-knowing strength and get down in the trenches with our sons. We have so much to offer them in our own experiences—our own trial and error—but we can't share it and it will never be received until we come down from the mountaintop and stop being know-it-alls.

Teachers: It's a powerful thing when teachers own up to their mistakes and confusion. By example, we can teach our students that being an adult is not about having all the answers, but about continuing to explore new questions.

Remember, Boys Need to Feel Understood

"For I don't know how many years, just about every conversation I had with my son ended with him screaming, 'You don't understand.' It made no sense to me, since I thought I was always talking about exactly the issues."

It sounds easy, doesn't it? After all, we're adults; we know how to listen, and how to respond with understanding. Then why is "You don't understand!" such a constant refrain from our boys? The answer is simple—when they are talking to you, and particularly when they are arguing with you, 90 percent of what they are saying is just words they desperately hope will convey what they are feeling. Growing up is not a rational process; it's almost exclusively an emotional experience, and what they are trying to tell you is how they feel, not what they think.

Yet we persist in hearing the words as some kind of rational argument that is usually woefully inadequate, and immediately jump into "clear rational thought" mode to help them understand the flaws in their logic. The problem is that it might have sounded as though they were attempting a rational argument (that is after all the form our boys are taught to use and respect), but it really wasn't.

What makes this particularly difficult with our sons is that they try very hard to put their words into logic form, but they desperately need us to crack the code and hear the feelings under the words. Our job is to understand them, and that means getting past the words and listening as deeply as we can to the feelings they are trying to convey, and help them to understand how they feel.

Parents: When your son starts in on a heated explanation of something, instead of getting caught up in the facts, ask a simple question, "And how did you feel when that happened?" That will at least get you—and him—pointed in the right territory.

Teachers: Make emotional language an important part of classroom discussions. Get beneath the story and talk about how the characters might have felt. This angle can breathe life into and help kids relate to any piece of literature, moment in history, or science concept.

Build Trust through Steadiness

"My father was a very mercurial guy. Depending on his moods, he could be incredibly biting and short with me or unbelievably open and loving. It used to mystify and hurt him that I couldn't switch gears that quickly. It took me some time to recover from one of his tongue-lashings."

I write a lot in this book about how hard it is to be a boy. What makes it even more difficult is that for the most part, just how difficult it is remains one of our dirty little secrets. As a society, we don't acknowledge it often, and for entirely too many of us, we don't even realize what an arduous and lonely path it can be. But there is another side of the story—it isn't easy trying to raise a boy, either.

The very same stressors that make growing up male so tough make raising a male child exceedingly delicate work, and in the process, we are all going to screw up over and over again.

One reason parenting a boy is so hard is that our mistakes often have consequences that go deeper and last longer than one would ever expect. When it comes to trust, boys can have a very thin line of tolerance. They are often so unsure of their position, and so tentative in their willingness to put themselves forward—particularly in the emotional realm—that after one cross word, one cry for help missed, one stretch of stressed-out work where we neglected to check in properly, our boys can become convinced that we don't care about what is happening with them.

That's why we need to try to be as emotionally steady as we can. It's hard for our children to learn to trust us when we're yelling our heads off one minute and then opening our arms to give a hug the next. Emotional steadiness is a beautiful trait, one that we can all cultivate by practicing thinking before speaking and taking time to cool off before dealing with a volatile situation.

If we damage our sons' trust, it can't be repaired overnight. We need to read the signs, put in the energy, and take the time to convince them that we are here, that we always will be here (even when we screw up), that we love them deeply, and that we do respect their feelings.

Parents: Learn to count to ten, to one hundred, or even to one thousand rather than lashing out. And if you do something to push your son away, do everything necessary to rebuild his trust. Open your heart and take your time.

Teachers: With all the stresses in today's classroom, do what you can to keep your cool. Give your kids the tools to develop their own emotional steadiness. Teach them how to deal with intense emotions—using either a time-out break, exercise, drawing, journaling, or singing.

Embrace Optimism

"My father used to sit me down every now and then and give me the 'hard cold facts of life' story. He grew up during the Depression, and to him life was just one long difficult struggle to survive. It used to scare me so bad I didn't want to grow up."

What with the media pouring each day's stories of tragedy and catastrophe into our homes, it is sometimes difficult to remember that the picture we are being continually given is extremely one-sided and painted a very deep black. The world certainly has its share of problems, but the things that are working, the places where life is blossoming and problems are being addressed, are growing dramatically.

It is important to try to give our sons the other side of the story—to let them know that there is great cause for celebration and optimism in the unfolding drama of our species. It is important because enough of the old distorted image of manhood still exists that our boys often feel the responsibility to be and do things that seem unattainable in a world that seems to be spinning out of control. Yet this is the world they are supposed to grow up into! Without an alternate view, and without a strong sense of hope and possibility, we put them at serious risk of giving up entirely before they have even begun.

Parents: Seek out what is working in the world and share it with your sons. At dinner tonight, tell them about all the changes for the better you have experienced in your life. Imbue them with a powerful belief in what can be done, and in the process, lift from their shoulders the burden of inheriting a world gone mad.

Teachers: For a current events assignment, insist that kids bring in a piece of good news. Introduce kids to the *Christian Science Monitor* and *Hope* magazine, two publications with positive slants on the world. Create good news yourself by starting a service project or a Random Acts of KindnessTM club.

Air Disagreements

"Half the time, when I was being disciplined, I'd end up sitting in my room fuming, because to me the punishment never seemed to fit the crime."

One of the great dangers in raising boys is allowing them to retreat too often into the solitude of their own minds. All the tides of tradition are already pulling them away from connection, and we need to make sure that we do nothing to encourage that drift.

One particularly sensitive moment is when we are disciplining our sons or when we have disagreements with them. God knows boys are going to get into their fair share of trouble, but it is crucially important that as the arbiters of right and wrong, we solicit their active participation in both the understanding of what is taking place and of any subsequent consequences.

That doesn't mean turning over control, but it does mean calmly helping them to understand all the reasons for our actions, asking for and respecting (even if we disagree) with their reasons for having done what they did, and then asking for their suggestions for appropriate consequences.

That also means being completely honest about our own feelings, not just assuming the role of jurist. I remember having one such conversation with my high school aged son about coming home late without a phone call to warn me. We were getting nowhere until I told him I was afraid something terrible had happened to him. That was all it took. He apologized, we hugged, and a conversation that was in the process of pushing us away from each other brought us that much closer together. More amazingly, he never again failed to call me if he was going to be late.

Parents: Always take the time to carefully explain your position during disagreements and discipline and practice the art of full disclosure—your worries are something he needs to know about. Never let a disagreement create distance between you and your son; instead, take it as an opportunity to get closer.

Teachers: Classroom discipline should be a two-way street as well. Make sure to take time to listen to the perspective of the "troublemaker." Develop consequences as well as commitments to new behavior together.

Practice Honesty

"My brother was always making up little stories to cover his butt. You never knew whether something he said was true or not. As a consequence, I lost all respect for him, and to this day don't quite believe anything he says."

We know that the truth is a powerful thing and that without it everything turns into a game of illusions, yet small boys often feel almost compelled to lie. Why? I think the answer rests in the space between expectations and reality.

More than girls, boys tend to have an image of themselves they want to believe is true, and when they fail to live up to this image, it sometimes feels easier to lie about it than to admit their failure. The barrage of messages they get about who they are supposed to be and how they are supposed to act is at times so overwhelming that they feel compelled to create for themselves an image that satisfies the expectations they feel. But it isn't real, and when they fail to live up to their own image, the only thing they can think of is to pretend they did.

As parents, we need to treat their lies with compassion instead of anger, while we teach them the importance of honesty. They are not "bad boys;" in lying, they are trying desperately if misguidedly to be good (or at least look good).

Most important, we need to teach them the illuminating power of honesty by practicing it ourselves, particularly in our dealing with them. When we make a mistake, the least we can do is admit it up front. Don't jump to excuses and defenses, but take the opportunity to show them the importance and value of honesty: "Yes, Officer, I was going forty-five in a twenty-five zone." "Yes, son, I did promise to make it to the game."

Your willingness to tell the truth no matter the consequences will help him learn the value of honesty.

Parents: One great technique to overcoming a child's tendency to lie is the old, "You won't get in trouble if you tell me the truth about what you did." Not only does it promote honesty, but it shows you value honesty more than perfection.

Teachers: Show the movie *Liar, Liar.* Talk about lying as well as making excuses, exaggerating the truth, and half-truths. Invite your students to think about what it means to be honest with yourself and others.

Seizing the Teachable Moment

"In high school, I had drifted pretty far away from my mother, and then I came home one day, and my mother came out to meet me in tears. Her mother had died. We stood there holding onto each other both in tears, sharing a sadness I can still feel. It's odd, but that day completely changed my relationship with my mother."

Life isn't scripted as much as we sometimes wish it were. Sure, we have our routines, and at times it seems like those routines just repeat themselves over and over again. In the midst of those routines we often go on autopilot—we've been here, done this so many times that we just go through the motions, and that may include our interactions with our children. But one of the responsibilities of being a parent is staying awake to the possibilities that life serves up, and the more we pay attention, the more opportunities we will discover.

A tragedy like a death or serious illness in the family or a major earthquake or flood always opens the door to discuss feelings and to connect on a deeper level. But even in the depths of the most ordinary day, something will emerge. It might be as small as a noticeable mood shift or a bad traffic jam caused by an accident. These moments are doorways out of the "business as usual" mode and into an experience of deep sharing, but all too often our reaction is exactly the opposite. It is odd, unusual, perhaps even frightening, so we shut down, not knowing what to do or say. Even upon the death of a loved one, it is possible to spend so much time being stoic we forget to share our grief and pain.

Seize the moments; every chance that arises in your life is a chance to feel deeper—to connect and bond in a way that will have lasting impact.

Parents: Look for one thing that happens today that might help you have a moment of connection with your son. Resist the temptation to back away just because it might be uncomfortable or you might not know exactly what to say. Be yourself and speak from your heart.

Teachers: The daily news provides us with enough bad news, so take the opportunity to turn it to a good use every now and then by having the class share their thoughts and feelings about events like earthquakes in Turkey or war in some distant country. Also, take time to talk about important events in your students' lives—the birth of a sibling, a friend moving away. It can bring everyone closer together.

Set Limits

"I realized partway through high school that while my parents were pretty strict with my older sister, with me, they had stopped enforcing the rules. I proceeded to get myself into more trouble than I could have imagined."

Children need rules and limits. Without them, life can be a very scary place, since children are ill-equipped to make decisions for which they have no foundation or experience. This is particularly true when they become teenagers. Yes, they are pushing the limits and trying to convince themselves they are "all grown up" and can make their own decisions, but they aren't and they can't, at least not without putting themselves at terrible risk. Yet we unconsciously treat our daughters and our sons differently, stretching to protect (and sometimes overprotect) our daughters while backing away from firm guidance with our sons in the mistaken belief that they need to go through this frightening gauntlet alone to become men.

Setting appropriate limits is essential. The rules will of necessity be ever shifting as our boys grow older and become more capable of making their own decisions. But that only means we have to become more engaged in discussing, negotiating, and enforcing reasonable rules and limits. It is helpful to remember when engaging in this difficult process that the absence of your participation will feel to your sons like an abandonment at the deepest level. At some level, they know that they need your guidance, and if it is withdrawn, it will feel for all the world as though you no longer care about them enough to help them.

Parents: Engage your son, particularly as he gets older, in the setting of the limits: What do you consider a reasonable bedtime? When do you think you should be home on weekends? While you may encounter unreasonableness, many parents who try this find their child's suggestions to be stricter than their own. And if he helps create the rules, he's more invested in following them.

Teachers: Discuss the benefits of good limits. Help them discover for themselves how and why boundaries on behavior work to give structure to our lives and freedom within that structure.

Model Empathy

> *"My favorite aunt was everybody's favorite aunt. She was one of those people who profoundly influenced every life she touched. She wasn't famous, or rich, or beautiful, but she had the ability to make you feel like you were one of the most important people in the world to her, and that everything you thought and everything you felt was fascinating."*

Empathy is the fine art of feeling another person's feelings. It is a source of incredible richness and one of the most powerful resources available to us. Unfortunately, it is also one of the rarest, particularly in men. That should come as no surprise, since men are pushed away from even rudimentary emotional skills, and it is a great tragedy because through empathy we are able to experience the broadest possible scope of emotional experience. By being able to feel the texture and sense the depth of another's emotions, by being there with them and offering our support and whatever strength we can bring to them, our own experience is dramatically expanded.

Empathy is the secret weapon in raising boys who will grow up with a deep emotional intelligence, so teach them well and teach them by being empathetic yourself. Always lead with your heart. Respond to every situation by first and foremost focusing on, acknowledging, and sharing your son's feelings. Whether it is the undifferentiated joy of youth, the anger arising from a fight with a best friend, or the sadness brought on by an illness, share the feeling, and luxuriate in this extraordinarily rich human emotional capacity. Accept the gift your children give you to go back and relive the raw emotional power of growing up by sharing in their feelings, and in the process, you will teach them the importance and value of our emotional world.

Parents: Besides modeling empathy, practice it with your sons. Ask them to imagine what it feels like to be deaf like the next-door neighbor, lose their house like the person in the fire on the news, or win twelve million dollars. The more they practice getting inside someone else's skin, the finer their empathic skills will be.

Teachers: When the opportunity arises either within the community of your school or even the outside world, teach empathy by having students try to put themselves in another person's position and articulate how they would feel.

Apologize, Apologize, Apologize

> *"One of my father's disciplinary requirements was that I apologize whenever I did something wrong. It was always the hardest part, not because I wasn't sorry, but because having to speak those words felt like a public announcement of how inadequate I was, and I felt like a complete failure."*

In general, it is much more difficult for a boy or a man to apologize than for a girl or a woman. It might be simply that boys and men have ingrained in them that they aren't supposed to screw up. We are supposed to be the modern version of the gallant knight who always operates from a place of honor, and an apology is simply an admission that you were not who you were supposed to be in the first place.

It may sound odd, but if your son has this difficulty, you can help him by apologizing every chance you get. Apologize for getting home late, apologize for not having the time you want to spend with your son, apologize when your stress level causes you to be curt or even just inattentive to his needs. The powerful double-barreled message that is encoded in any apology is that we are all human and we all make mistakes, and that you, my beautiful son, mean so much to me that I don't want another minute to go by without you understanding how sorry I am for my behavior.

Parents: The power of apology cannot be underestimated. Psychologists claim a good apology has three parts:

1. A sincere expression of regret: "I am sorry I was late to your recital."

2. A truthful explanation for your behavior: "It just completely slipped my mind."

3. An offer to make restitution: "How about if we go out for ice cream after you're done?"

Teachers: Have students remember a time when they didn't get an apology for something they felt they should have, then write a story of what they wished had happened. Talk about the power of apology to heal old wounds.

Sprinkle Love in Your Day

"When I was really young my father used to tell me bedtime stories. He made up a whole world of characters who lived in a place where everybody loved everybody but still things were always getting messed up for a while."

Love is central to our lives. It defines our relationship to our children. It makes us happy. It gives us the courage and strength to do the right thing, and it is the one thing more than anything else we would wish for our children. So why don't we spend more time talking about it than we do? We tend to just assume it's understood, but instead it becomes one of those mysterious subjects that never emerges into the light of day. It might be partly because love is so powerful and, certainly for many of us fathers who weren't raised with the benefits we want to pass onto our sons, it is a whole language we aren't that good at speaking.

No matter our gender training, most of us could use more love in our lives. So start practicing! Celebrate the love you feel by talking, by sending love notes, by bringing home a treat for no reason except you care. Become an evangelist of love, and let your son share in the beauty and experience of how love works in daily life.

Parents: In addition to telling your children over and over again how much you love them and why, talk about why you love your good friends, the things you love about your spouse. Invite friends and relatives to share their love stories with your family.

Teachers: Ask students to write essays about someone they love. Help them explore more deeply the love in their lives and the people, old and young, for whom they feel it.

Stick with It Even When It's Tough

> *"My parents love to tell my kids about the three years their father barely said three words. It's become part of our family lore. And it's true, I just withdrew into myself for quite a while, but my parents hung in there and just kept on talking to me like I wasn't being a complete jerk."*

Growing up is hard, and sometimes the way our sons respond is just to shut down and pull away. They even get surly and cynical as a way to erect a defensive force field around themselves. It can be frightening to watch your sweet young boy suddenly turn into a silent film horror monster, but it shouldn't be all that surprising. How is he supposed to deal with social expectations that are impossible to attain, build an identity when nobody seems to be able to tell him how to do it, deal with emotions without the experience or tools necessary and that he isn't even sure he's supposed to be having, and by the way keep Mom, Dad, teachers, coaches, and friends happy? Temporarily giving up the field suddenly doesn't seem so strange.

What we need to do when these moments arise is ride them out with him. Let him have his retreat, but keep reminding him you are there, caring and ready to help. Try to intuit what is going on (I know it can be pretty tough when there is no communication going on, but you'll be surprised what you can figure out if you start paying close attention), and venture into his territory in as subtle and nonthreatening a way as possible.

Sideways communication is often best at these times. For example, if you think one of the things bothering him is not fitting in at school, you might out of the blue one day tell him, "I ran into an old friend today I haven't seen since high school, he and I were the 'out group' as opposed to the 'in group.' Boy, were those hard days."

Obviously, the story you tell depends on what your instinct tells you are his issues and where you can bring yourself into his story, but the point is to tell the story on yourself. Don't even try to include him. When he's ready to volunteer something he will, but by sticking with him, trying to read the tea leaves of his mood, and creating opportunities for him to engage, eventually he will.

Parents: Silence can be one of the hardest things to endure, but it is also when he needs you to hang in there the most.

Teachers: When a student in your class seems to have shut down, acknowledge his presence even when he doesn't respond. Reach out with a note, a casual touch, a kind word. Know that what he is going through may have little to do with you.

Can the Internet Help Boys Develop Emotional Intelligence?

At times, social media can provide opportunities for a boy's social and emotional skill development in ways that face-to-face interactions do not. By engaging with social media, boys can of course do a lot of the things that they like to do in real life, such as finding new friends, deepening their connections with family members and existing friends, brainstorming with others, and sharing basic aspects of their lives in words and/or pictures. The internet, including both social media and multiplayer games, also has the potential to level the playing field for some boys with special needs; for example, a boy who has difficulty picking up social cues may learn about social interaction online and use readable visual clues such as emojis to discern others' emotional reactions to his posted content. [Parents may wonder how they can tell if their son needs help with reading social cues and other skills for social interaction. One of the best ways to do this is to compare him with other boys his age—not just his own friends, but others in his grade at school. How easily do they make friends of any gender? Compare how they do with just hanging out with peers or engaging in conversation. Also, discussing this question with your son's teachers or perhaps parents of his classmates may be of value.]

But wait, there's more: According to research published in the journal of the American Academy of Pediatrics,[1] online engagement can also allow boys to develop themselves and explore further aspects of life and interaction with society.

Social media participation also can offer adolescents deeper benefits that extend into their view of self, community, and the world, including:

1. Opportunities for community engagement through raising money for charity and volunteering for local events, including political and philanthropic events

2. Enhancement of individual and collective creativity through development and sharing of artistic and musical endeavors

3. Growth of ideas from the creation of blogs, podcasts, videos, and gaming sites

4. Expansion of one's online connections through shared interests to include others

1   O'Keeffe, G. S., Clarke-Pearson, K, & Council on Communications and Media. (2011). The Impact of Social Media on Children, Adolescents, and Families. *Pediatrics*, 127(4), 800–804. DOI: doi.org/10.1542/peds.2011-0054. Online version retrieved March 14, 2020 from: pediatrics. aappublications.org/content/127/4/800.full?sid=4f54b3cb-d54c-4671-85db-38034f238ec9

from more diverse backgrounds (such communication is an important step for all adolescents and affords the opportunity for respect, tolerance, and increased discourse about personal and global issues)

5. Fostering of one's individual identity and unique social skills (The Impact of Social Media on Children, Adolescents, and Families)

This is all just meant to get you started on brainstorming how you might potentially encourage a boy toward such development and exploration using the internet.

Some boys on the spectrum may have a deep interest in one or more specific fields of knowledge (for example, dinosaurs, cryptography, ancient calendars, or the history of dice). For such a boy, a blog of his own may be an excellent way to express his interests and perhaps have the opportunity to interact with others who share his interests.

CHAPTER 4

Helping Him Navigate the World of Emotions

Big boys don't cry. This is the signature statement of how we have raised our boys for centuries. And in denying them their tears, we have unwittingly cut them off at a very tender age from the entire world of healthy emotions. Big boys don't cry; they grow up to be men who have precious little understanding of their own emotional centers. That is a handicap even more devastating in its effects than losing one's sight or hearing, for only our feelings can lead us to the essential truth about ourselves.

When we raise sons without access to their own emotions, we deny them the whisper of their deepest wisdom. Within the incredibly intricate, complex, and confusing path of life, this capacity for knowing is our greatest gift. Yet instead of nurturing this gift and training our boys in its use, we have largely allowed it to wither and recede into the background.

Without access to this miraculous tool, our sons grow up like carpenters without saws, trying to fit all the pieces of their lives together without the ability to cut, shape, and size the materials they are given. They operate by someone else's design, and the results can only be the construction of a life that does not reflect who they truly are.

Show Your Love in a Way He Can Receive It

Loving our children is easy; figuring out how to communicate that love is more difficult; and doing it on a consistent basis is more difficult still. Part of the problem stems from our own unarticulated sense that with a love so strong, somehow the children should just "know." They don't, and particularly with boys, the ways they can receive love will change over time. Sometimes, when they are young and still unspoiled by the mantrap our culture sets for them, the words themselves are enough. Often, as they get older and are struggling with the different images of what they are supposed to be, our sons need more than words; they need us to do something that can only come from our love for them. It could be simply talking to them, without lecturing and with heart wide open. It could be taking time out of our busy schedule to spend with them.

It could be sharing something special with them and them alone.

What works will shift and change over time, and it is our responsibility to shift and change with it. It is the parents' responsibility to remind their sons on a regular basis both how precious they are and how important it is never to stop communicating that love. Both messages are crucial because our sons need every ounce of our love to give them the strength and courage to grow into emotionally healthy men. At the same time, the nature of growing up male in our society is that you are constantly being pressured to shut off the connection to your emotions. Parents who model for their sons the ability and importance not only of maintaining that connection but communicating it regularly are the best examples they will ever have.

Parents: Make communicating your love for your son in whatever way he can receive it at the moment one of your highest priorities.

Teachers: Invite kids to journal about how they know that someone loves them. How do they express love to others in their lives? Explore the many ways love can be expressed.

Don't Guess, Ask!

> *"A woman friend of mine offered to cut my hair one day,
> and as I was sitting there on the back porch, she ran her
> hands through my hair very gently, and out of nowhere,
> tears started to fall from my eyes. In that instant I suddenly
> remembered how my father used to do that when I was very
> small and how wonderful it had felt. As I grew up, he stopped
> doing it, and I had never realized how much I missed it."*

Communicating love the way our boys can receive it is not
always easy because we don't always know what they want,
and it hardly ever occurs to them to tell us. The range of
things that can mean love is as broad and varied as our
imaginations. It could be hugs, special gifts, appreciative
notes. It could be praise, but maybe only praise about
certain things. It could be time together doing nothing.
It could be the quiet sharing of stories, thoughts, and
feelings; it might be reading together, playing together,
taking walks together.

The possibilities are endless, so ask. Otherwise you might
never learn. Be specific and keep asking until you get an
answer. Then keep asking again and again as they grow,
for just like you, their needs and wants change. Put what
you have learned into practice, but at the same time
don't overdo it. Communicating love is a precious act and

should be done often but not routinely. The honesty and specialness of the moment must be preserved.

Parents: Make it an ongoing responsibility to discover the things that make your son feel loved. Ask, "What are the things I do or can do that make you feel loved?" Sometimes he will have a hard time answering, so explore more deeply. "Can you ever remember really feeling how much I love you?" Or, "Do you recall any time when you felt really safe and peaceful, when for that moment everything seemed to be exactly the way it should be?"

Teachers: Encourage your students to write notes to a special adult by finishing the sentence, "I know you love me when..." Students and adults may be equally surprised at the responses. (Make clear that it is up to the students whether or not they share what they write with that person.)

Do Things Together

"I remember when I was little my dad used to spend lots of time with me, building things, playing catch, kicking the soccer ball around, but somewhere along the line he just kind of faded away. I don't know if he got too busy or what, and it took me a long time to even realize how much I missed doing things together, but by the time I became a teenager it was like we lived in different worlds."

There is an old adage that says, "Men do, women are."
Like most gender assumptions, there is a kernel of truth to
this. Much more than with our daughters, with whom we
can have a conversation about feelings, if we want a freely
flowing emotional connection to our sons, in which we can
openly explore their feelings, we need to *do* things with
them on a regular basis.

Traditionally, boys build their emotional connections
to others through activities. Whether this is a genetic
predisposition or simply centuries-old learned behavior
will undoubtedly remain unclear for years, but the
consequences are clear: Boys generally connect with
others most easily by doing things together.

And we need to be the ones who initiate the doing.
Because of old but still powerful stereotypes, boys are
both less ready to articulate emotional disappointment
and more willing to act "tough" by accepting your lack
of participation without complaint. It may seem a small
thing, but the combination of culturally induced resistance
to discussing feelings and the equally strong cultural
admonition to be "strong" can create gaping holes of
disconnection into which our boys can easily fall and from
which they do not know how to escape.

With today's accelerated pace, it may be hard, but find
a way to do something with your son on a daily basis;

after all, in the final analysis, few things will ever be as important as your children. Live that importance by remembering that what we want to do and what our intentions are do not matter nearly as much as what we actually do.

Parents: Be scrupulous about creating specific things to do with your son. And that means more than watching his Little League game (although that's good, too). Give yourselves a chance to interact directly through action.

Teachers: In the press of state-mandated curriculum, much of the classroom time is taken up sitting, listening, and responding, and very little time is allocated to doing. Try to redress this imbalance, and when you are able to do so, put the bulk of your focus on the boys, because it is here they can receive and accept your support.

Teach the Language of Emotion

"It used to irritate me when my wife asked me how I felt, both because I was not really sure how to figure it out, and because even if I had some sense of how I really did feel, I could never find the right words to communicate exactly what it was."

Our language is rich in words of emotion, but if you ask most people to start listing words that describe feelings they will rattle off a half dozen or so—angry, sad, disappointed, frustrated, happy, joyful, and, yes, they almost always start with the negative ones—and grind to a halt. So review the partial list below and think about times you had these feelings. Then start today to expand your own emotional vocabulary.

Safe, relaxed, satisfied, undesirable, lethargic, needy, confident, optimistic, loved, insulted, resentful, ignored, excited, energized, connected, empty, trapped, obligated, amused, fortunate, effective, rotten, infuriated, idiotic, empowered, spirited, peaceful, puzzled, resigned, terrified, special, wonderful, vibrant, regretful, intolerant, gullible, respected, fantastic, elated, hesitant, horrible, hated, eager, excellent, engaged, indifferent, inept, invisible, tremendous, tipsy, tingly, lonely, lousy, lost, forgiven, funny, fearless, grumpy, guilty, gullible, enthusiastic, enriched, empathetic.

Parents: Sit down after dinner one evening and together with your kids come up with every word you can that describes a feeling. Post the list and add to it as you think of new words.

Teachers: Choose a word or two from the list, discuss its meaning, and after some reflection time, invite students to share when they've felt that way.

Respect His Feelings

"One of my most painful memories of growing up were the times I would be trying to tell my parents how I felt, and they'd say, 'You shouldn't feel that way.'"

Sounds simple, but it isn't. His feelings are exactly that— his feelings. They are real, they are true, and they are a precious gift when shared. But they can also be difficult to hear without becoming defensive ourselves, so we need to resist pulling out all the tricks we have developed over time to deflect and negate the feelings.

Just as an example, your son says to you, "You don't love me!" It's absurd, and your automatic response system wants to kick in with, "Don't even say that," or "Of course I love you," or "That's ridiculous." But each of those answers sends the same message in differing degrees: "Your feelings are wrong or stupid." And in that moment, we are the ones who are wrong because we completely ignored what he was feeling and jumped instantly to our own defense. In the process we send the more damning message that we don't want to hear about his feelings.

Feelings are never wrong; they simply are. They may emerge from a misunderstanding or a failure to properly communicate, and at times they can be inappropriate or misplaced, but they are always true. We need not only treat them with respect but be thankful that in this one place in our lives we can always know that the truth is being spoken.

Parents: If we want our sons to be able to express their emotions, then we need to nurture and cherish every opportunity to do so. Whenever your son is trying to communicate a feeling, whether in words or behavior, stop everything, open your heart as wide as possible, put yourself in his position, and try to respect what it is he is feeling. Remember that this is a precious moment.

Teachers: Practice digging deeper when an emotion is expressed rather than trying to deflect it or defend yourself. If a student expresses boredom or confusion, ask, "What goes on in your mind when you're bored?" or, "When was the moment you began to feel confused?"

Respond to His Feelings First

"It took me almost thirty years to realize that I had developed a very bad habit of ignoring other people's feelings completely and jumping immediately to what I perceived as 'the issue.' I know it sounds pathetic, but it never occurred to me that the feelings were the issue."

Respecting his feelings is the start; responding immediately is the next step. Getting our sons to express their feelings is difficult enough; the very least we can do is be meticulously careful to respond immediately and compassionately to those feelings when they are offered. Surprisingly, many adults stumble over this, with potentially devastating results. Often when boys do build up the courage to express their emotions, it is because the feelings are so strong that they simply have to come out. In many of those situations, the feelings are not well articulated and not at all what we want to hear. Our job is to sift through all the accusing or hostile words, find the core of his feelings, and articulate them back to him whether you like them or not.

When your son tells you, "You never listen to me!" what he is really saying is, "My experience is that you don't really listen to what I am trying to say, and that hurts." The issue that needs to be dealt with first and foremost is his feeling—he is hurt. Address the feeling before going on to the issue that may have provoked the feeling.

Parents: Respond to his feelings with compassion, and then work your way back through his perception before you get to your own response. An example would go something like this: "I can see that this hurts you and I'm really sorry. Hurting you is the last thing I would ever want to do. I can see that you feel like I don't listen to you, and I really do want to understand what you are saying, but obviously I'm not doing a good enough job of that. What can we do to fix this?"

Teachers: So much misbehavior has deep feeling underneath. Ask students in trouble what feelings led to what they did. Receive the feelings and take them into account rather than moving too fast to punish.

Teach Him to Take Responsibility for His Feelings

> *"I used to think emotions were something people imposed on each other. In my house, it was always 'You make me so mad,' or 'I'm so disappointed by you,' or 'Your mess is driving me crazy.'"*

We are so poorly trained in the language of emotions that even when we use the right words, we rush past the feeling to instantly assign blame to the "creator" of that feeling—"You hurt my feelings!" After all, if I feel hurt, then certainly someone must have made me feel this way! What gets lost in this presumptuous conclusion is everything of any substance. In the first place, more often than not the person being accused of "making you feel hurt" never had any intention of hurting you. They may have said something or done something that they should have known might hurt you, but simply didn't think of the consequences. Then again, they may have done or said something that they had no idea might hurt you. It is rare indeed that they purposefully tried to hurt you, yet that is the stinging message they receive back.

In the second place, remarkable as it sounds, no one can "make you" feel anything. Your emotional response is your own responsibility—what angers one person might embarrass or even please another. One significant component of emotional intelligence is taking responsibility for one's feelings. Help your son learn the difference between how he feels and what in fact has happened.

Parents: Avoid sentences that start with "You made me feel" or any variation thereof. Help your boy get to the bottom of an emotional exchange by learning to explain calmly the effect the other person had—"When you laughed at what I said, I felt hurt and misunderstood"—and allow the other person to explain or apologize.

Teachers: Effective conflict resolution should begin with each person "owning" how they feel. Sometimes writing or drawing before speaking can help those involved get to the ability to articulate "I" statements that indicate what part in the conflict he or she was responsible for.

Plan Quiet Time

> *"The church we belonged to had an annual retreat for*
> *teenage boys, and my parents used to make me go every*
> *year. I always resisted because it seemed hokey to me, but*
> *in retrospect it was a great experience. It was one of the*
> *only times I was forced to do nothing and just sit with my*
> *own thoughts."*

One of the prevailing myths about boys, and particularly adolescents, is that they spend too much time alone. They disappear behind a closed bedroom door and don't reappear for hours, and then emerge only to wolf down food and return to their inner sanctum. But don't confuse private time with quiet time. Both are necessary, but quiet time is much harder to come by. For the most part when our boys are holed up in their rooms, they are fully occupied, listening to music, banging away on the computer, talking to friends on the phone, reading, building something, drawing, or whatever. Getting them to understand the importance of real quiet time can itself be a challenge but one that is well worth it.

Real quiet time requires being in a place with minimized distractions. By cutting out as much external input as possible, the deeper part of ourselves can emerge. The yearnings of our hearts become more clear; our thoughts and feelings (after an initial period of racing around at light speed, confused by all the silence) begin to slow down and can be seen more clearly.

Structured retreats can be very beneficial. I used to take my son wilderness camping, and we would spend a few hours each day off on our own just basking quietly in the embrace of nature. Organizations like Outward Bound provide a great mixture of team building and quiet time. Real quiet time is difficult to organize around the house because of all the existing distractions, but even that can be done if planned properly.

Parents: Make the effort, even though it may be resisted, to give your son regular periods of quiet time. We all need to clear out the distractions of life now and then to rediscover who we really are, and it can be an invaluable experience for our growing boys.

Teachers: Time for quiet reflection built into the school day can aid long-term learning. Plan just fifteen minutes of "unwinding" each day, and notice what happens to students' ability to concentrate.

Allow Him to Express in His Own Way

"When I was younger, I used to rock back and forth when I got excited. My mother would always tell me to cut it out, but

> *my grandfather loved it. He said he liked it because he could*
> *instantly tell how excited I was."*

We live in a world that values words, preferably expressed
in a calm, rational manner. There is much to be said for
that ability, but we can get so focused on channeling
all our boys' energy into that one narrow outlet that
we dampen and miss out on other expressive ways of
communicating with us. When they come running up to
us talking a mile a minute, hands flying all over the place,
excitedly pacing or rocking, or maybe dragging their feet
and hanging their head, resist the temptation to get them
to cut to the chase and "tell us" what's up.

Stop for a moment and observe the way he is expressing
his feelings. Often, particularly when boys get into
noncommunicative phases, this will be the only evidence
you have of what is really going on inside them. Become a
master of interpreting clues that can reveal the feelings he
may or may not be willing or ready to express. Celebrate
his expressiveness because it can help you understand him
better and because it is a natural part of his own fledgling
attempts to let his feelings show.

Parents: Start with words or actions that acknowledge what
you already know about how he is feeling—a hug if he looks
sad; "You certainly seem happy," or, "I love seeing you so

excited!" if he is bursting with joy. Acknowledge, reinforce, celebrate, and then get to the news.

Teachers: Explore body language with your students. Start with socially recognized gestures like a wave or a shrug. Then allow students to think about their friends, parents, and other family members and share any gestures they know that express feelings without words, like, "My brother Larry stands on one foot when he's nervous."

Use Sports to Get at Feelings

"The best times I spent with my dad were watching sports. We would get all excited, laugh, scream at the television, argue over penalties and what was the best strategy. During the game there was this almost cocoon-like energy, and as soon as the game ended it would dissipate."

It doesn't take a team of scientists to tell us that most boys are sports crazy. What would be nice is a little research on why. Is the need for sport and competition bred into us? Is it a socialized way to maintain our hunter-gatherer skills, or is it just an instinctual need to play? It's probably a bit of all these, but my own theory for why sports has become almost an obsession with boys is that it is a safe place where they can uninhibitedly experience and express their feelings. You can love your team, get passionately excited, and be bitterly disappointed at a close loss, saddened by a season-ending injury, or brought to the heights of joy by a game-winning home run or touchdown.

With sports, boys are *expected* to fully engage their emotions, screaming at the top of their lungs or jumping around high-fiving their friends. In a culture that pressures men to repress their feelings, sports are the socially accepted outlet in which men can be emotional. The sheer numbers of passionately committed sports fans are a good measure of just how desperately we need more venues to be our emotional selves. However, since sports are venues, encourage your son if he has a passion for sports and help him transfer that experience into the rest of his life.

Parents: Help draw out the feelings boys have for sports and extend them to other situations. Ask questions like, "Can you imagine what it must feel like to work so hard to accomplish something and then have it fall apart because of an injury?" or, "When have you felt so excited about something in your own life?"

Teachers: Make space in the classroom for the discussion of important sporting events. Have kids roleplay pivotal moments to experience the feelings of the players for themselves. Invite them to roleplay similar scenes from their own lives.

Look Beyond the Anger

> *"I went through a two-year period when I was about thirteen when I was angry all the time. It was like a vicious whirlpool that kept sucking me down further and further. It seemed like I was angry at everything and everybody, which of course just made everyone else—especially my parents—angry and exasperated with me."*

Anger is one of the few emotions we allow our sons. Sadly, it is even expected, a poisonous but inevitable male characteristic. But male anger is not bred in the blood. It is instead simply the emotion of last resort when all other emotions have been forbidden. When boys are cut off from expressing the full range of emotions, their sadness, disappointment, insecurity, and confusion gets squeezed down into a jumbled stream of seething anger. This is a predictable consequence of raising our sons in a way that does not give them the opportunity to experience and come to grips with all their feelings. Ultimately, it is the source of virtually all the rage and violence that tears at the very fabric of our society—angry men blindly striking out at anything and anyone.

Anger is the loudly ringing bell that can alert us when our sons have begun to disconnect from their other feelings. When anger erupts, we need to get beyond the hard edge of that emotion and discover what lies behind it. It is not always easy, since anger often shuts down dialogue, but crossing that abyss is exactly what we need to do. On the other side are deeper emotions that have been left untended and unexpressed.

Parents: When your son is angry, do not reply in kind, even if the anger appears hurtful and completely unjustified. Instead search for a way to soften the anger of the moment so you can begin to follow the threads back to its origin. This may take days, even weeks, of patience, empathy, asking, listening, and waiting, but it is worth the effort.

Teachers: Anger in the classroom is both disruptive and unacceptable. Do what is necessary to defuse the situation, but make an effort out of class to extend an empathetic hand. A public eruption of anger will frequently be accompanied by a feeling of shame or embarrassment. By letting him know that you are more concerned for than upset with him, you will create an opening for him to begin to discuss what is really going on.

Play with Feelings

"My parents really restricted TV-watching in my house. I resented it at the time, but thinking back, I realize that a lot of the creativity I now use in my job—I'm an art director—came from all the hours I spent drawing and dreaming."

Children play—thank goodness, or we would never get anything done! But children's play has a point; they are practicing all kinds of emotional, social, and intellectual skills. We have long known that children's play prepares them for the different stages of their lives, but we have been slow to turn this wonderful laboratory to its best use. In a sense we allow our children to dictate how, when, and what they will play, and some of that is good in that it can allow their own creative needs to be met. But we need to start paying attention to their play and participate both in the play itself and in the direction it takes.

More and more frequently we have abdicated this fertile ground to the television. Children are easily captured by stunning video images, whether it be Barney or the Power Rangers, and their play takes on a decidedly directed and sometimes unhealthy bent.

One area that is almost completely neglected is playing at emotions. If we want our boys to grow up in touch and in control of the emotions within them, it would help if we gave them some early practice through play. There are at least two components of emotional intelligence that kids can learn through play. One is to identify the feeling: I'm mad; I'm frustrated; I'm excited. The other is what to do about the feeling: I'm going home; I'm going to tell you how I'm feeling; I'm taking a walk.

Parents: Play a game where you take turns positing "How would you feel and how would you act?" questions that the other person must act out: "How would you feel if you came home and found your sister had broken your fire truck? What would you do about it?" "How would you feel if your best friend told you his family was moving to Portland? What would you do then?"

Teachers: Have kids brainstorm school-related "sizzle points"—moments when feelings are high and decisions need to be made. Pick several ideas, and then explore options in small groups. Notice how many different feelings and actions can come from any one situation.

Deal Effectively with Tantrums

> *"I had a terrible temper when I was younger, and it would just seem to come out of nowhere. One minute everything was fine, the next minute I was out of control and in the doghouse. Once I even punched a hole in the wall of the living room."*

When our sons suddenly erupt into temper tantrums, our almost automatic response is to come down on them fast and hard. That kind of behavior *is* unacceptable. Our response comes partly from the shock that our sweet boy could suddenly turn into a monster and partly from fear that he won't learn how to control these outbursts.

At these times, it is important both to bring the situation under control and to teach him that there are more effective ways to express anger. But at the same time, we need to see these outbursts for what they really are, an eruption of emotions that he has obviously been holding in and not dealing with and resolving. If we discipline the outburst without also taking the time to explore what caused it and without helping our boys to recognize and articulate their negative emotions in a constructive way, the message we send them will only reinforce the cycle of repressed emotions and inevitable outbursts.

Tantrums are a strong warning sign that our sons have entered that dangerous zone where their ability to understand and effectively deal with the strong emotions that accompany growing up is not functioning properly. Our job is to intervene immediately and with as much compassion as we can muster. We need to see these outbursts as nothing more than cries for help, and we need to be there to provide that help. We need to teach him safe ways to express feelings, and we need to notice his emotions before they reach the boiling point.

Parents: When your son has a temper tantrum, do what you need to calm him down, allow some time for the heat to cool off, and then focus on what caused the outburst. Remember, he's not a bad boy, he's scared and doesn't know how to handle the strong feelings that are racing within him.

Teachers: Help kids tune into how they are feeling by setting a timer to go off every hour. Instruct them to notice and write or draw how they feel. At the end of the day, discuss the kinds of feelings they noticed and how it affected them to notice them so often.

Teach through Other's Mistakes

"I love my older brother, and one of the reasons I love him so much is that he paved the way for me through the confusing years of growing up. I got to watch him make his mistakes, stumble, and screw up; it helped me figure a lot of things out."

Learning how to take responsibility for our mistakes is something that even the best of us sometimes have trouble with. None of us is eager to admit that we spoke too quickly, too harshly. None of us wants to be exposed in our weakness, having caused someone else discomfort because of our own mistake.

For small boys facing the unrelenting pressure to be good, be strong, be someone they can't possibly be, taking responsibility for mistakes is painfully difficult. Even when they do, they are usually too mired in feelings of inadequacy and shame to pay much attention to more subtle messages about how to better navigate this difficult terrain.

Often the best opportunities we have to help them hear and listen occur when they aren't the ones in trouble. Kids especially love to hear about when you screwed up as a kid. It makes them feel they don't have to be perfect. So make use of siblings' and your own stumblings to take some of the pressure off and to explain how you or they could have dealt with the situation better in the first place.

Parents: Any mistake is a learning opportunity, and with our sons, sometimes the mistakes of others (including our own) are the best learning opportunities. Take every opportunity that comes along.

Teachers: Collect stories of famous people who "blew it" before they succeeded, like Babe Ruth (the strike-out king) and Thomas Edison (kicked out of school). Think together about what each person might have learned from his mistakes enabling that individual to go on and succeed.

His Emotions Aren't All about You!

"Growing up, every time I acted up, my mother took it as a personal insult. I finally learned it was just easier to bottle it

all up than face the consequences of being blamed for making
her miserable."

"How could you do this to me?" How many times have you
heard these words? How many times have you yourself
said them to your son? If you are like most people, the
answer is more than you would like to admit. All of us
sometimes slip into the self-centered position of thinking
that everything is about us, but it is a very damaging
role to assume, particularly when dealing with young
boys who are struggling to understand and express their
own feelings. When our son stumbles, acts out, or gets
angry, we need to focus on his feelings and find out what
is going on in his heart and mind that has brought on
this behavior.

By shifting the focus onto our own disappointment or
anger at his behavior, we not only abandon him right at
the moment he needs us most to help him understand
his motivation, we send him the dangerous message that
his mistakes and outbursts are responsible for our pain.
And by sending that message, whether we want to or not,
we are telling him to shut down emotionally—all that is
acceptable to us is a perfectly in-control boy.

Raising an emotionally intelligent son means supporting
him in the unpredictable and mistake-ridden journey
through his emotions. To be his guide, we need the

maturity and resilience to allow our own reaction to recede in importance. Even if his behavior was intended to upset us, as it sometimes will be, our taking center stage as the injured party only reinforces his inappropriate way of expressing anger or frustration. It does nothing to help him figure out how to let us know more appropriately that he is upset with us about something.

Parents: If we encourage our sons to express their feelings, there will be plenty of times when they do it very badly. Our job is to work with what they give us, to help them retrace their feelings and reframe them in a way that is clear and appropriate. We can't do that if we turn all the attention onto our own feelings of hurt or disappointment.

Teachers: Teachers as well can take misbehavior too personally, as if our students don't care. Acting out or poor achievement need to be explored individually to discover the feelings and motivations beneath them.

Give Their Feelings Room

"I grew up in a house where emotions were flying around all over the place. Both my parents were very volatile, and my sister and I learned that to get any attention at all we had to stage a major drama."

Despite all the sweet talk about caring and concern for feelings, most people are incredibly bad at demonstrating care and concern in the moment. We gravitate to our own feelings, latch onto them like a life vest in a turbulent sea, and completely disregard how the other person is feeling. That's why so many disagreements end up with us figuratively curled up in the fetal position in our own corner, astonished at the lack of love and concern being displayed by our partner.

Such behavior makes for a rocky and ultimately distant relationship, but the one place we have absolutely no right to behave in such a juvenile manner is with our children. The rule of thumb when dealing with our kids is that it is *their* feelings that matter, not ours. Each of us is supposed to be the adult, the guide who will help them understand and navigate this world. We can't do that unless we put all the focus in the right place. They will undoubtedly do things that hurt us, that disappoint us, and that make us angry, and they need to know it when they do, but not until we have effectively explored their emotional experience.

When kids are faced with parental volatility, one of two things happen: either they learn to become hysterical themselves to get attention, or they shut down altogether because there isn't any space for them to experience and express their own emotional reaction—they're too busy trying to avoid yours. Both can have serious consequences, although the behavior of a hysterical child is more overt. I once knew an adolescent who didn't tell his mom he was being molested for a year because he didn't want to deal with her hysteria.

Parents: In the world of emotions, the old adage "The customer is always right" needs to be reframed for parents. Your children's feelings are always more important than yours. Deal with them first, fully and compassionately, and then and only then let them know how their behavior affected you.

Teachers: Teaching is a highly emotional profession, with so many feelings in the classroom besides your own. Seek help if you need it in a support group or counseling to keep yourself clear and able to attend to the kids' needs at school.

Help Him to Grieve

"When I was twelve, my grandmother died. I was devastated because she was such a safe harbor for me. Nobody ever told me not to cry, but everyone was just walking around feeling sad and trying not to show it so I thought that was what I was supposed to do."

Emotions exist for a reason: to be experienced so that we can learn more about the deeper parts of ourselves.

When we shut that experience down, we not only turn our backs on vital information that could enrich our lives beyond imagination, but we also build a wall around a part of our inner beings, a wall that blocks us from conscious understanding. The more often we do this, the less access we have to the very information we need to live our lives consciously. After years of repressing emotions, our interior landscape becomes a clutter of unknown obstacles, and our conscious decisions start to drift into shallow parody, cut off from any real information about who we are and what we need.

The stronger the emotion repressed, the more damage we do to ourselves, and it is hard to imagine an emotion more powerful than grief. Yet, the very power of that feeling often stops us in our tracks. We know intuitively that to truly experience grief might mean losing control, collapsing in a sobbing fit of tears that will feel for all the world like a never-ending spiral into despair. If we are lucky, we learn that experiencing grief, in all its painful intensity, will not harm but heal us, and ultimately it will deepen our understanding and appreciation of life itself. It is a lesson that is very difficult for a young boy to learn on his own, but it is a gift of extraordinary importance that we can offer him.

Parents: If your son must deal with the loss of a loved one, lead him through his grief with the deepest possible compassion. Hold him, cry with him, grieve with him, stay by him, and let him work his way through this painful experience at his own pace, but always let him know you are there and supporting him. And don't be embarrassed to show him that you are suffering too, but be sure to give him all the room he needs for his own feelings.

Teachers: The expression of grief sometimes has its place in the classroom. If a student suffers a loss, it's important to make room for the tears and the compassionate sharing of stories of loss from our own lives.

Learn His Body Language

"I could never figure out how my mom always knew how I was feeling. I'd walk in the door and she'd say, 'Bad day at school, huh?' Usually I'd deny it, but once I asked how she knew, and she took me out to the park across the street and starting pointing out people and telling me what she could tell from their body language. It was really eye-opening."

We all know that many people show their feelings through their body language, but we don't talk about it or use it as the invaluable teaching tool it can be. Talking to boys about emotions can sometimes meet with a brick wall,

but when we shift gears slightly and get them engaged
in trying to interpret feelings from body language, it
can become an engaging game with long-term benefits.
Slumped shoulders, shuffling gait, scowls, leaning forward
when someone is speaking, the movement of eyes, hands,
and arms may give us reliable information about how
someone is feeling.

The more attuned boys become to body language, the
more the world of emotions is brought into their lives.
It also gives them information that allows them to be
more considerate and empathetic and gives them a
way to raise issues that might otherwise be difficult or
awkward for them.

When using this technique, it's important to help kids
understand that their guesses might be wrong. Not
everyone shows their feelings in their bodies, so boys
need to learn both how to guess and to check out their
assumptions—for example, crossed arms might just be
comfortable for someone and does not necessarily mean
they are hostile.

Parents: Take your sons out to public places and practice
identifying the range of emotions you see. Get your son to play
detective and put into words the emotions at play and maybe
even make up stories about what could be going on. (But make
sure you all know that this is just speculation and needs to be

checked out if it is being done about someone you know.) You can even do this watching television, but you'll miss out on the storytelling part.

Teachers: Do roleplay exercises without words to encourage students to read a person's body language and figure out what's going on. Have fun learning this important skill.

Teach the Difference between Feeling and Acting

"I was the kind of kid who felt something and just did it. Boy, did I get in trouble!"

One of the hallmarks of emotional intelligence is impulse control—thinking before acting. Like other aspects of emotional smarts, boys tend to have more trouble with this than girls. It can get them into all kinds of trouble when young and may lead to difficulties with drugs, alcohol, and violence.

A key component of impulse control is understanding the difference between feelings and actions. Just because you feel something doesn't mean you should act on it, and understanding that truth goes a long way toward creating good impulse control.

Help your son understand that feelings exist outside our conscious control. They just are—they arise and fall in an ongoing flow: frustration, elation, sadness, anger, hurt, joy... They get triggered in us by the intersection of the outside world with our personal histories—that's why the same thing that makes you cry may have no effect on me. We've had different life circumstances.

Whether or not to act on a feeling—to tell someone you're mad or stomp off in a huff, for example—is a choice. You don't actually *have* to act on any feeling. Sometimes it's better not to. We need to teach our sons that just because we feel something doesn't mean we have to *do* anything about it. What's best is to first notice the feeling, identify it, and then think about whether acting on it is a good idea.

Parents: Humans always feeling something all the time. Start the process with your boy by doing what author Daphne Rose Kingma calls "The Four Winds of Feelings." Ask him, "What are you sad about? How do you know you are sad? What are you happy about? How can you tell you are happy? What are you angry about? What are your body sensations? What are you excited about? What are the sensations with that feeling?" This will help him label his emotions and understand they are always there.

Teachers: Help kids learn from their mistakes. Have students think about times when their feelings got the better of them and they acted impulsively. What were the consequences?

What do they want to remember to help them the next time their emotions build?

Help Him Learn to Handle His Feelings

"I never knew what I was supposed to do with all that I was feeling. That's why I try as much as possible to not feel anything."

Most of us were never taught about the arena that social scientists call "managing feelings." What they mean by this is not "management" in the traditional male mode, which is repression and denial. Rather they mean knowing what to do about strong emotions. Do you collapse in tears? Allow the feeling to move through you? Tell the other person? Seek help from others? Decide to distract yourself instead?

The truth is that all of these (and many other) choices are appropriate under different circumstances, and yet many of us aren't even consciously aware that we have any choice at all! The first thing we can do is let our boys know that there are a variety of healthy responses to feelings, and give them a list. Here are some: Write a letter you never send expressing how you feel, act out your feeling with your body, go into a room alone and scream at the top of your lungs, take your feeling for a walk alone, or call a friend and ask him or her to listen without saying anything.

We can't help our sons feel the full spectrum and intensity of their emotions without giving them some tools to deal with them.

Parents: Here's a great way to process any feeling: Do an abstract drawing. Get some crayons or pastels and a blank piece of paper and simply draw the energy of your feeling. This even works with little kids—show me how you feel on this piece of paper. And try it yourself! It doesn't matter what it looks like.

Teachers: Do roleplay exercises of heated situations in which kids make different positive choices in dealing with their feelings. Help them practice alternatives to lashing out before the crucial moment arises.

Cultivate Emotional Insight

"My teenage son is quite good at seeing the patterns of his behavior—the other day he told me he seems to have a problem relating to girls. I guess he got that from me. I'm always analyzing everything."

Insight is yet another dimension of emotional intelligence. Insight is the capacity to perceive the nature of something. Emotional insight allows us to identify patterns in our emotional reactions and, by perceiving the patterns, to have more choices in our reaction.

Instead of just freaking out, for example, every time you see a big dog coming down the street, thus treating it as a random and isolated event, with insight, you are able to think, "Oh, I guess I'm afraid of big dogs. I see I do this every time one comes along." Once you have that awareness, the pattern has less effect on you. Next time a big dog comes along, you can think to yourself, "Here's that thing again that scares me." Recognizing that often helps alleviate some of the panic. With maturity, you can even go further and analyze why you are afraid and what other choices you have as to how to react.

People without emotional insight go through life as if every day were their first day on the Earth, making the same mistakes again and again and never realizing it, much less taking responsibility for them. I once had a friend who had been married four times—twice to an alcoholic, once to a gambler, and once to a compulsive eater. When I asked her if she saw a pattern to her relationships, she looked at me dumbfounded. Until she could see her attraction to addicts, she would continue to pick addicts to marry. Insight allows us to learn from our emotional mistakes and to correct them. Help your boy begin to thread together the emotional patterns of his life.

Parents: First see if you can recognize a pattern in any of your son's feelings—that he gets terrified when he has to speak in public, for example. Then when the occasion arises again, ask him if he's noticed this problem before. Help him see the pattern and discuss alternatives.

Teachers: Open a discussion about fear and courage that will help students understand that these two emotions usually go hand in hand. Have them name a time when they were afraid. What frightened them? How did they find the courage to move through it? Did they talk to themselves? Take action? Imagine it being all right and then make that happen? Help them notice their patterns of success.

Teach Good Stress Management

"My father worked like a dog and dropped dead of a heart attack when he was fifty. Stress management? He would have laughed at the concept!"

Good stress management is one of the components of emotional intelligence. It requires an awareness of feelings—of overload, for instance—and then the willingness to take action to deal with the feelings.

No wonder men have historically been bad at stress management, opting instead for alcohol, outbursts, and overwork. Many of them don't even know they are feeling anything! Many of the healthy things people can do to deal with stress—yoga and meditation, to mention just two—tend to predominantly attract women.

If we want sons with healthy EQs, we need to help them recognize when they are feeling stress and learn positive coping mechanisms. One way to do so is to ask how they are feeling before some stressful event—say a big test at school or an important ball game.

Merely asking how they are feeling usually won't get you very far. Help them to tune into the body sensations that might indicate stress—a clenched jaw, butterflies in the stomach, a generalized sinking feeling—so they begin to recognize their body's unique signals. Then help them learn some relaxation techniques for tense situations.

And be sure you are practicing good stress management yourself. They're watching!

Parents: Here's a simple relaxation technique they (and you) can do anytime. Sit quietly, inhale, and tense all the muscles in the body. Then exhale, letting all the tension drain away. Slowly take three breaths in and out, being aware of nothing except the breath coming in and going out. You can even say 'inhale' on the in-breath and 'exhale' on the out-breath.

Teachers: Who says you can't teach this same technique to your kids? It takes five minutes to learn at the most.

CHAPTER 5

Supporting Him in Resisting Stereotypes

Wanting to raise our sons to be fully integrated and emotionally healthy men is not enough. Even if we were to do our parts perfectly, we are not the only influence in their lives. Our sons are growing up in a world that is embedded with centuries-old assumptions about what it is to be male. The cumulative mass of our history will tug on our boys with a powerful pull that no small boy can resist on his own.

It is encoded in our language and in the stories we tell. It emerges in the classroom, on the playground, in the locker room, in gatherings of small boys and young men. It pours out of our televisions and movie theaters. It is ubiquitous and pervasive, surrounding them with worn-out and dangerous images of our society's expectations of men. In incremental pieces, it builds up into a mountain of

pressure that pushes them further and further away from
their hearts and into the one-dimensional vacuum that is
our cultural legacy of manhood.

If they are to have any chance whatsoever of resisting that
pressure, we need to be there with them every step of the
way, explaining, deflecting, protecting, and supporting
them to find a healthy way to grow and develop.

Engage Early!

> "When my son was three, he went through this prolonged
> phase of identifying everything and everyone by gender.
> A group of friends would stop by and he would suddenly
> announce, 'There are four boys and three girls here!' He even
> started assigning gender, according to some mysterious
> criteria in his own mind, to neighborhood dogs and cats."

The time when our children first become aware that there
is a difference between boys and girls is a precious one,
and our usual reaction is to watch with delight as their
minds start figuring it out. But it is also an opportunity
for us to begin laying the foundation that will help them
resist the onslaught of gender stereotypes that will soon
descend upon them. It's easy to miss this opportunity
because the process used to assign gender roles and
attributes is transparent. We don't have special classes in

which our children sit down and go over a list of male and female characteristics. Instead, we have nursery rhymes like, "What are little girls made of? Sugar and spice and everything nice. What are little boys made of? Snips and snails and puppy dog tails." We as parents provide examples as we act out our gender roles, and television programming floods our children with superficial images of what men and women should be.

The net result is a very powerful multichannel barrage that takes place on an almost unconscious level. It can be frightening to realize that our sweet babies are being brainwashed into taking on gender attitudes and behavior without our participation.

So when your children start noticing the differences between boys and girls, engage them immediately! This is easy, since they are already fascinated (if ignorant) about what this all means. Talk to them about the range of human expression and let them know that the more positive characteristics they can develop the better—tough *and* tender, considerate *and* focused. Don't shy away from explaining the more traditional roles society has defined—they will be bombarded by these images anyway, but make the effort to let them know your opinions. Why, after all, can't girls be focused on what they want, and why can't boys have their own variety of sugar and spice and be just as nice?

Parents: The sooner you start engaging your boys in this discussion, the better they will be for it. Don't leave this crucial step in their development up to the boob tube.

Teachers: What a great opportunity to engage our youngest students in an exploration of how and why we as a society allocate gender roles. This could be a lesson plan for all time; it already meets the first criteria for learning: your students are totally fascinated with the subject.

Tell Him He Doesn't Have to Be Strong

"My father was from the John Wayne school of parenting— shut up, don't complain, and be strong. That was my idea of what being a man was all about."

Why does a man have to be strong? Is life a weightlifting contest? Are we still preparing for doing battle on some medieval battlefield with fifty-pound broadswords? *Strong* is a word we should retire from usage for a few generations until it has lost some of the charge it now carries. Real strength is a beautiful thing, but it can only grow from inside, from a deep understanding of ourselves. It is employed not to dominate, but when we need it, to help us live our lives with integrity.

Telling small boys to be strong is telling them everything in one word that they do not need to hear. We usually say it when they are faced with some challenge or some difficulty—you fell off the horse; now be strong and get back on. Your favorite uncle died, but be strong and put away the tears. It reminds them that they aren't strong physically, emotionally, rationally, or in any way; they are just small boys still trying to learn what it means to be alive. Telling them to be strong gets immediately translated into telling them to stop feeling what they are feeling. In effect, you are telling them to cut themselves off from the fear, the hurt, and the confusion they may be feeling and retreat into their own disconnected silence.

Parents: Remove the word *strong* from your vocabulary when talking about your sons.

Teachers: Study this word with your class. Find out its derivation. Explore its many meanings. What more specific descriptions could replace it? Expand your students' awareness of this powerful yet debilitating word.

Face Bullying Early On

"The first fight I ever got into was my very first day of school. This big kid started pushing me around and calling me

names. I pushed back, and the next thing I knew, we were both in the principal's office getting chewed out."

What comes to mind when we think about kindergarten and first grade? Maybe it's all those adorable little kids milling around, or maybe it's our own concern about how well our child will handle the separation or how well he will fit in. What we tend not to think about—but should—is that particularly for our boys, this is a precarious time: Our sons are moving out of the supportive environment of the home and into a world that is already primed to enforce an emotionally suppressing boy culture. A friend of mine who teaches first grade jokingly calls her class "The Wild Kingdom," but left unaddressed, there is nothing funny about an environment where bullies are allowed to operate and where some boys are teased and made fun of for looking different, for having glasses, for being small, or for no reason at all.

And if you think that is an overstatement, consider a recent study done through Wellesley College. It found not only that bullying and teasing are frequent occurrences in most schools, but that virtually all the bullies were boys, and most distressingly, that in most cases teachers did not intervene. Even under the best of circumstances, such behavior is difficult if not impossible to stop, and it can become a formative influence. Girls who are teased or bullied rightfully feel and react as victims. Boys who are teased are more prone than other boys to feel weak, to be ashamed of their own perceived inadequacy, and to feel already—at the age of five or six—"unmanly." So young and already being taught that they have to be tough, show no fear, and closely guard their feelings lest they become the next target! And the boys doing the bullying have already learned that violence is the male way to solve problems—a very dangerous if prevalent attitude.

Parents: Get deeply engaged in your son's school life. Talk to him about what goes on. Talk about teasing and bullying and how harmful and disrespectful it can be. Make sure you know what is going on so you can be there to encourage and support him in staying true to his heart.

Teachers: This is well trod but difficult territory. It is hard to both teach a class and deal effectively with bullies, but know that deflating the effect of teasing and bullying as well as turning it around by making kindness a core class value are both essential to the emotional health of the boys in your class.

Teach Conflict Resolution

"When I got mad, I hit. That's what my dad did to me, and that's what I learned to do. It got me in a lot of trouble as a kid. Finally, I learned to stuff how I felt and walk away

because I didn't want to be like my dad. Now I explode
verbally instead. I'm not sure that's all that much better."

Not many of us know how to handle anger well. We
haven't had good models. If anything, the models have
gotten worse, as kids learn from adults around them
as well as from contentious radio and TV shows that
screaming and not listening to one another are the ways
to deal with conflict. And if that doesn't get you what you
want, a fist, a knife, or a gun will.

It is up to us to teach our boys a better way. They need to
see us handle conflict maturely, and they need to be taught
explicitly how to do it themselves. If we're hotheads,
yelling at them or at our spouse (or God forbid, hitting or
throwing things), then that's what they're going to learn.
If we're conflict-avoiders, passively going along and then
doing what we want behind the other person's back, they'll
learn that, too.

How do you handle disagreements? Is it the way you
want your child to learn? If not, perhaps you should
read a good book on anger. Learning how to deal with
anger in a healthy way is a precious skill that we and our
children need.

Parents: Here's a great technique taught by many schools that you and your kids can practice. It's called "Traffic Light" and can be adapted for any age. Something happens to upset you: That's a red light. It's time to stop and figure out how you are feeling. (This helps with impulse control.) You decide you're mad (or hurt or disappointed). Now the light turns yellow. This is the time to consider all the options for responding to your feelings and the consequences of those options. For example, you could tell the other person that you are hurt; you could hit them; you could yell, "I hate you;" or you could walk away and ignore them for a while. Play out the scenarios in your mind for each one: If I hit, I might get hit back, and then we'd be in a bigger fight. If I say, "I hate you," maybe he won't play with me again. If I ignore him, maybe he'll want to play later. Then it's green light: Choose the best option and notice what happens.

Teachers: Train older kids at your school to be peer mediators, and allow other children to go to them for support in conflicts. You'll provide good practice for the mediators and excellent role models for everyone else.

Counteract Pack Mentality

"When I was in junior high school, I got involved with a group of guys who were always getting into trouble. It was our way of proving something; we were out there rebelling against the system, whatever that was. One time, we got caught and my father had to pick me up at the police station. I was scared he was going to kill me, but instead, when we got home, he

> *just looked at me and said, 'Why are you doing this? This isn't who you are.'*"

Boys lose themselves easily. The more removed they are from knowing how they feel, the more easily they can lose themselves in the projections and pressures of a peer group. If you don't have any clear sense of who you are, of what is important to you, then you seek that meaning somewhere else, often in the comforting reassurance of a group. This lack of awareness is the internal hole that can make for wild behavior shifts, hanging out with a "bad" crowd, or even joining gangs. The group tells you what to consider important, how to dress, how to behave, and most important, tells you that you belong.

As parents we have the advantage, for the truth is our sons would much rather belong in our family than anywhere else. But it is our responsibility to make sure they feel that. We need to create and maintain a constant emotional connection, a continuous supportive and compassionate environment where they know that every part of them, even their own perceived weaknesses, belongs and is loved. We also need to practice the other suggestions in this book, for the more our boys are in touch with their deepest wants and feelings, the less they will need to follow the crowd.

Parents: Pay close attention to your son's emotional barometer, and remember that the pull of our culture is always trying to undermine his confidence in understanding and dealing with his emotions. Get connected and stay connected—you are the taproot for his positive growth.

Teachers: Make explicit the challenge we all experience living in community of how to be ourselves and yet join with others. Discuss what important beliefs and values each person has that he or she wouldn't give up to be part of a group. Talk about what values a group worth joining might have.

Watch for Guns

"My fourteen-year-old son's best friend was accidentally killed by his younger brother while fooling around with their father's gun. My son would have been there that day, but he was grounded."

Guns are everywhere. Just because you don't have one doesn't mean your boy is safe. Other kids could bring them to school, and other families have them in their homes, not always properly locked up.

The ubiquity of guns is a reality in today's world, and we shouldn't hide our heads in the sand about it. You should pay close attention to your son's possible interest in guns when young, and you should teach him that a gun is a very dangerous weapon. He should know that kids should not play with guns under any circumstances, and that he should let you know if he sees a gun at a friend's house. Some parents go as far as to ask the parents of their son's friends if they own guns. If the answer is yes, their child is not allowed to visit.

Some parents decide purposely to teach their sons to shoot under controlled circumstances, like at a firing range, so that the whole mystery and allure is diminished. Others ban any contact whatsoever.

No matter what we do, however, we can't be absolutely sure that our sons won't be around guns. Ultimately, we need to rely on their good sense and emotional intelligence to get out of a dangerous situation. And we increase our chances that they will exhibit that good sense if we reinforce again and again that the measure of a man isn't found behind the barrel of a gun.

Parents: Acquaint yourself with gun violence statistics and establish a dialogue with your son about guns. Have him rehearse what he would do if he saw a friend with a gun.

Teachers: Talk about recent shooting incidents at schools. Explore the feelings that might have led to this behavior. Imagine how the boys involved in the shootings could have

handled their feelings if they had no access to guns. Find out
from your students how they honestly think these situations
could have been prevented.

Encourage Friendships with Girls

*"Growing up, my best friend was a girl named Becky. She
played a mean game of baseball, which helped, but what
made that relationship so special was that when I was with
her, I felt like I could just relax and be myself. With a lot of
my guy friends there was always some level of jockeying
for position to see who was smartest, most clever, most
outrageous, faster, a better hitter, or whatever."*

What better way to learn the potential richness of both
the masculine and feminine sides of ourselves than to
explore them within the confines of a close and trusting
relationship? A number of recent studies argue that as our
children grow older, their friends exert more influence
on both their behavior and their sense of identity than
do their parents. What is not clear is how much of this is
related to how many parents seem to pull away from their
children as they grow, particularly their sons, but we do
know that encouraging healthy cross-gender relationships
can open up a whole new world for our sons.

If we were anthropologists trying to understand the roles and behavior of a tribe, we wouldn't just hang around with the guys. If we did, we'd end up with a distorted picture, and that is exactly what happens to many of our sons growing up. Years of tradition, conditioning, and misplaced fears have created a culture where boys and girls tend to withdraw behind gender lines very early, in the process losing the extraordinary opportunity to be exposed to a much broader and richer experience. Recently that seems to be changing, at least at the high school level, where at least some boys and girls are resisting the pressures of dating to be "just friends."

Parents: Go out of your way to encourage your son's friendships with girls. Talk about friends of the opposite sex who have been or still are important in your life.

Teachers: When doing class assignments by group, resist the temptation to put girls with girls and boys with boys. Create opportunities through workgroups and project teams for boys and girls to experience working together.

Teach Real Independence

"My father used to tell me all the time that I needed to be independent. Now I am; my life is focused around what I

want to do when I want to do it, and part of that includes
spending very little time with him. I know how I got here, but
I also know something is really wrong with this picture."

Independence is a big-time male theme. Be your own
man; don't be tied to any apron strings; keep your own
counsel; and don't let anyone in too close or you might
lose your independence. The theme has deep roots in
this country, and it has tragic consequences. For the
kind of "independence" that boys are pushed into is not
independence at all, but isolation and disconnection.
Ultimately it leads to a life that is nothing but a
shallow illusion.

Although the "strong silent type" is celebrated in a
constant stream of movies and stories, it is in fact the most
pathetic role any human being could ever adopt—cut off
from any real meaning, disconnected from any real feeling,
apart from any true community; so independent that for
all practical purposes, he doesn't exist in the stream of life
other than as a self-focused actor.

Real independence means having the strength,
understanding, and wisdom to live your life deeply,
fully, and with integrity regardless of what others think.
It means having the courage to expose yourself—to risk
the deep waters of life that can only be experienced in
connection to others. It means to live continually and

fearlessly from your heart, from where you can experience the incredible richness of life. It means recognizing, celebrating, and holding on to your uniqueness while at the same time sharing it as completely and constantly as possible with others. Help the boy in your life learn the difference.

Parents: Celebrate Independence Day by reminding your son that real independence is not about isolation and mere control of one's outward life circumstances—it is about living his life with as much honesty, integrity, and depth as he possibly can.

Teachers: Create opportunities for your students to share their interests and experiences. Help them explore their uniqueness and how their individual gifts can make them resources for each other.

Teach the True Meaning of Respect

"My grandmother was a remarkable woman. One thing she taught me was never to judge others harshly. Once I had said something cutting about a guy in my class, and she stopped me in my tracks and told me that since I was not in his shoes, since I had not lived his life, I had no right to condemn him."

Respect is another concept that trips males up. Much violence these days occurs when some boy feels he has been "disrespected" and decides to take out a gun to solve the problem. It's easy to realize that such behavior comes from a deep sense of insecurity, for if a young man felt truly comfortable with himself, it wouldn't matter to him what other people thought.

But respect is an important concept. When we think of respect, we usually associate it with people of great accomplishment, but that is not respect. We might admire what they have accomplished and believe that they handle themselves well, but real respect goes much deeper and should be universally dispensed. Life is infinitely complex, and every one of us has had to walk our own path. At any point in that journey, we may falter, we may make mistakes large and small, or we may act unkind or unappreciative, but the how and why we got there is our problem, and we are the ones who will pay the price for our mistakes.

Real respect encompasses the deep compassion we should hold for every person regardless of their circumstances. It is an important lesson to pass on to our sons, because in the competitive male world, it is far too easy to fall into angry, judgmental behavior and to treat other people disrespectfully. Help him also to understand that those who might "disrespect" him are worthy of his compassion too, for they are so insecure that they can't do anything else.

Parents: Have a conversation with your son about respect—
what it is and what it is not. Help him see that respecting others
is the compassionate position, but that going to war over
"disrespect" is counterproductive.

Teachers: Respect for others' choices is especially important in
school, where cliques can foster false assumptions and conflict.
Have a class discussion about what it means to act respectfully
toward others who have different viewpoints and lifestyles.

Don't Get Hung Up on Respect Yourself

*"Once when I was a teenager, I was arguing with my father
and said something like, 'That's the stupidest thing I ever
heard.' Wrong thing to say to my dad. He blew up at me and
sent me to my room for a couple years, and we hardly spoke
for almost six months."*

Like the boys themselves, it's easy for fathers and sons
to get drawn into silly battles over honor and respect;
after all, this is traditional, heavily loaded male territory.
For generations of men, honor and respect were the
main benefits of all their hard work, sacrifice, and
accomplishments. Largely cut off from the world of
feelings, love, and support, we simply did what we were
supposed to do and were in turn respected and honored.
Within that framework, anything that smacked of

disrespect was experienced as a full-frontal attack on our very worth.

It's a difficult legacy to shake, but particularly with our own sons, who are young, inexperienced, and destined to make mistakes by the handful, we need to temper our own sense of injury and remember that we are adults. It is our job, not theirs, to find a way through this minefield.

Growing up male in this age is extraordinarily difficult. The old rules don't work any longer, and the new ones are still in the process of unfolding. It is small wonder our sons are frightened, confused, and at times angry with us. And no matter how unartfully they may express themselves, it is our job to help them make some sense out of it all. We cannot do that if our first reaction is defensiveness that forces them even further away.

That doesn't mean you have to put up with insults or inappropriate barbs; it just means that you need to deal first with the issues that underlie the attack, and then calmly let them know that there are more appropriate ways to express their anger.

Parents: When your son's anger erupts, don't rush to the "Don't you dare talk to me that way" conversation-ending response. Anger can be very difficult to deal with, but it is coming from somewhere. If we are to stay connected to our sons and help them learn how to deal with their emotions, we need to put aside the harsh words for a moment and focus instead on what is really going on.

Teachers: Sometimes students don't know that how they say something has a tone of disrespect. Roleplay different ways of saying the same thing until students can recognize the ones with a disrespectful edge. Then, in the midst of an angry encounter with you, remind them that you can hear them better when they speak in a respectful tone.

Give Him Real Role Models

"My parents had a good friend who visited us two or three times a year, and they were very special times for me because this man was not only really interesting (he was a working archaeologist), but he was also a very real person. What amazed me was that he took an interest in me and treated me as if I were something special even though I was just a kid."

The importance of role models is something we all understand, but it is getting more and more difficult to find them for our boys. Men in public service offer us better examples of how not to live than how to live; the great explorers of past days have turned into extreme sports participants whose main talent is putting themselves at risk; sports heroes may be gifted athletes, but the overcommercialization of sports has given us more self-promoting millionaires than men of character.

Even personal role models are getting more difficult to cultivate as the increasing speed of life spins us into what seems like an increasingly isolated single-family existence with fewer and fewer opportunities to expose our sons to men of real character. But the need for our boys to be around positive role models is more urgent than ever. At a time when the very definition of manhood is changing, how better to give our sons the rich material they need to fashion their own definitions than to expose them to men who have successfully walked this path before them.

Parents: Boys need men in their lives! Be constantly on the lookout for men of depth that you would be proud to have your son emulate. Search out these men, talk about the things that make them special, and let your son experience them.

Teachers: Do a lesson on role models. What is a role model? What characteristics do you feel are important in a role model? Have students bring in pictures and stories about people they admire and explore why these are people they look up to.

Beware the Anti-Mentor

> *"I played football in high school. I loved the game and for the most part had a great time, but my coach was a complete jerk. His idea of instilling character was by berating everyone. After we'd lost a big game, he showed up at practice the next day with box full of skirts and forced us all to practice in them."*

Study after study has demonstrated what a powerful character builder team sports can be. In recent literature, participation in team sports has been singled out as one of the most effective ways young girls can maintain a strong sense of their own self-esteem, and it is equally clear that team sports can help boys experience a broad range of emotions. It's an opportunity to test yourself, to stretch your abilities, to experience all the emotions that accompany setting goals, working hard, making progress, succeeding, faltering and failing, and picking yourself up again, and all within the context of a closely bonded team. But all that can be not only undone but turned into a negative if the coach imposes his own twisted sense of manhood on his team.

Fortunately, the "take no prisoners" type of coach is gradually fading away as greater awareness of the character and importance of team sports emerges. But there are still plenty of Neanderthals out there, and as parents we need to be very aware of the methods and attitudes employed by anyone who is in such a powerful position relative to our sons. Make sure you are aware of what's happening on the practice field and in the locker room, and be supportive of both your son's participation and his need and right to be treated with respect. If necessary, don't be afraid to do whatever you feel is necessary to protect him from this kind of male abuse.

Parents: Coaches can be a great blessing in your son's life, but bad ones can be as dangerous as land mines. Make sure you know as much as possible about how your son is being treated in these situations. Talk to him about what is right and what isn't, set good boundaries, and support him in enforcing them.

Teachers: You are often in the best position to notice when coaches or other school-based mentors are crossing the line and treating students in ways that undermine the boys' self-esteem. If you notice any danger signs, don't hesitate to raise them in the proper forum. There is no excuse for disrespectful treatment of young men.

Stop the Glorification of Violence

"I remember watching a movie on television with my son when he was eight. It was one of those 'loner good guy versus a whole gang of bad guys' movies that moved from one scene

of good triumphing over evil through violence to another. I
hate to say it, but we watched the whole movie even though I
kept thinking, 'What am I teaching him?' "

A recent study by a children's advocacy group, Children
Now, found that boys' favorite entertainment were movies
and television shows that showed violence as the "heroic"
way to solve problems. This was true even though the boys
(aged ten through seventeen) viewed the protagonist as
"angry" and "violent." As shocking as it is, the results can
hardly be surprising. The only emotion we truly allow our
boys is anger, and when the message they grow up with
is that they must win—the girl, success, money, power,
status—or be deemed weak losers, the results are almost
inevitably violent.

The models they grow up with are the expanding inventory
of "shoot 'em up" computer games and movie heroes
such as Bruce Willis, Sylvester Stallone, Jean-Claude
Van Damme, Wesley Snipes, and whoever else might be
playing the latest version of the emotionally suppressed
male avenger. These models are dangerously damaging,
but they flood the airwaves and we allow our children
unfettered access to them.

Trying to stand between our sons and this barrage of
violence is no small undertaking. "It's just a movie." "It's
fun!" "I like it." It may at times feel like you're standing at

the floodgates, foolish for thinking you can have any effect at all. But we need to do something and do it now to at the very least counteract the poisonous messages conveyed. We, with our adult perspective, may know it's just a movie or a TV show, but our small sons are getting a very different picture, and it is our job to correct the message before it is too late.

Parents: Have the courage (and it will take courage) to dissect the underside of this part of our cultural legacy. Our sons need to know that the violent avenger is not a proper role model for a man. Take the opportunity to explain that men have often been trapped in a prison of anger and violence, and that it is a prison that serves no one.

Teachers: Take a critical look at violent TV programs and movies with your class. Set up a debate about whether or not violent programming causes violence.

Talk about Sex

"I think my experience through puberty was probably pretty common. One day I was a little boy, and then all of a sudden, there was this sex thing taking over my mind and body, and the only people who ever said anything about it were my equally confused friends."

We all know we're supposed to talk about sex with our children. But just in case you needed it, there is an important reason to talk to our boys about sex that is not usually discussed, and that is to help them to understand that strong feelings are not supposed to be hidden in a closet somewhere.

When boys go through puberty, sexual desire, particularly in our highly sexualized culture, can rise to surging peaks that feel at times almost overwhelming. The important word here is *feel*. It is a distinctly physical sensation, but it is so much more. When as parents we tiptoe around the subject, pretending it doesn't exist, we not only fail our sons in their need to understand this powerful gift, but we reinforce the age-old message that anything associated with "feeling" is not to be spoken about!

And we are delivering this message at a time when our sons most need our help. The results are often a general emotional shutdown. How many parents have you heard complaining that their sweet young boy went through puberty and turned into a silent, sullen creature? One of the long-term dangers of abandoning our boys to a silent sexual emergence is that sex and emotions can get tied up together in a confused, distorted, and shame-filled package that results in men whose only avenue to emotions at all is through sex.

Parents: Yes, this is difficult territory, but crucially important. We need to raise our boys in an emotionally shame-free environment if we want them to grow up with access to and the ability to manage their own emotional maturity. Start talking about sex long before it becomes necessary; it makes it easier both for you and for them.

Teachers: Sometimes adolescents will talk more easily about sex with knowledgeable adults who are not their parents. If you can't play this role, find out who in your school can and send students with questions their way.

Help Them Learn Sexual Manners

"When I was in high school, I had a steady girlfriend I was crazy about. All my friends teased me constantly because we weren't 'doing it.' She wasn't ready, and the truth was neither was I, even though my body certainly said otherwise; but the pressure finally got to me, and I started to become much more insistent. The relationship ended in an ugly mess, and I regret my behavior to this day."

It can be difficult to talk to our children about sex because we are all very conflicted about it. It is probably fair to say that as a species we are in the midst of a long transition from sex for survival to sex as sacrament, and unfortunately the full range of impulses, desires, rationalizations, and understanding disturb us daily. It is all the more important that we talk to our sons about this confusing process, for without us, they will at some point in their growth be caught up in the evolutionary surge of hormones without whatever wisdom we can offer.

As a culture, we view young men as sexual predators— often telling our daughters that they will lie, cheat, steal, manipulate, and generally do anything they need to in order to get laid. It is a brutal and cynical viewpoint that like all modern myths, is based on elements of truth. But we need to focus precisely on the ways that it is harmful and untrue.

At the core, our sons are good and beautiful people with all the capacity and desire to treat women with the respect and care they are due. It is this aspect of our sons we need to nurture, without pretending or avoiding the difficult challenges they will face when confronted with their own powerful, emerging desire.

There is nothing simple and unambiguous about sex, and what they need from us is both our wisdom and our compassion. Teach them that sex is a two-way street, where the needs and wants of *both* people need to be considered. Explain to them that *no means no*, whoever is saying it.

Parents: Teach them to treat women well sexually—to take their feelings into account as well as their own. And of course, teach them to be responsible about sexually transmitted diseases and the possibility of pregnancy.

Teachers: After many decades of struggle, sex education seems finally to have found its place in our educational system, but don't let it become simply a clinical discussion of human anatomy. Build into your program discussion of the power and meaning as well as the uses and misuses of sex.

Encourage His Creativity

"I think I was lucky growing up because my mother loved to paint and she was always inviting me into her studio from the time I could barely walk and putting pastels and paints and chalk in my hand. The truth is I didn't inherit any of her talent, but I had a great time."

One of the things we often unconsciously do to our sons is restrict their world to the sphere of the narrowly physical and rational. We expect them to run around and play, and we expect them to think and rationalize, but we rarely encourage their intuitive creative side, which is one very powerful way to help them access the deeper parts of themselves. Whether it is writing, music, drawing, painting, or creating constructions out of various materials, encouraging them to make something where nothing exists gives them permission to open channels that are too often left unused.

It has long been known that the process of creating taps into parts of ourselves of which we are often unaware. It gives room for unconscious images and impulses to emerge without being filtered through the rational mind. The more often we utilize these channels, the wider the highway becomes and the better we become at bringing our creative and intuitive selves into our daily lives.

Think of it as a different language, a symbolic language. Most of our focus with our sons is on the language of words and, since we couldn't hold them down even if we tried, the physical expression of play. But without active encouragement of their creative side they can lose touch completely with their deeper, more symbolic encoded languages of creation.

Parents: Keep all kinds of creative materials on hand and schedule some "creative time." You need to do it, too, else it will feel too much like a chore. Sit down as a family on Sunday morning and draw what a dream felt like, or fashion something out of clay that represents how you feel at the moment.

Teachers: Integrating the arts into classroom lessons can enhance the retention of concepts and help students think more broadly and creatively. Using drama, the visual arts, music, and movement also invites more engagement in subject matter and could expose kids to sources of deep pleasure and self-expression that they'll use their whole lives.

Nurture the Connection between Brothers and Sisters

"When my son and daughter were little, I used to think all they ever did was fight, until I quietly looked in on them one morning and found them eagerly cooperating in some game they had made up. I realized the fights were all for my benefit. Left on their own they got along great."

Some of the worst aspects of gender stereotyping take place extremely early, and they are quite unconsciously caused by sibling rivalry. Let's face it, most children will do anything to get the upper hand in parental attention and empathy, and that includes using every distorted gender trick in the book to get their way. "She's such a baby!" "Mom, he hit me!" How many times have you heard some version of these complaints? While their purpose is to get you on the complainer's side, the effect can ingrain foolish one-dimensional stereotypes.

Don't get sucked into this game. Make sure no one is truly getting hurt, and if not, let your children sort out their own problems. You can make them bring the solution back to you to make sure it is fair but require *them* to find the solution. That way you not only undermine the gender games but give them the experience of learning how to work together and how to have a relationship that works.

Don't just let your sons' and daughters' relationships with each other take their own course. Engage yourself in trying to bring them closer and keep them closer together.

Parents: Create situations where they have to do things together, like putting up the campsite, making a joint Christmas present for Grandma, or cooking a family meal. It will not only enrich their relationship with each other (which will pay off enormously in the long run), but it will make it much more difficult for them to drift into their private boys versus girls camps as they grow older.

Teachers: When class projects need to be done in teams, make sure that boys and girls get mixed in together. Try to avoid classroom competitions divided on gender lines. Make up mixed teams for spelling bees or math games.

Help Them Deal with Fear

> *"I was scared of a lot of things when I was growing up, and my father's best efforts to help only made matters worse. He'd tell me to 'be a man,' and then he signed me up for boxing lessons—another thing to be afraid of."*

Fear is a powerful emotion, one that can be very debilitating unless faced head on. We all experience fear at different times and about different things, yet our boys grow up convinced that they are supposed to be fearless. In the language of small boys, to be fearless is to be a man, and that is a burden they should never be saddled with.

If you don't believe how deeply ingrained this message is, just think about how boys are always challenging each other, daring each other to do stupid or even dangerous things—rock fights, jumping off buildings, climbing tall trees, drag racing. A good part of the culture of boys is centered around determining who is tough and who is chicken, and the message is bluntly simple: If you are afraid, you aren't one of us.

But fear is a very useful survival mechanism, and we need to help our sons learn that fear is a normal, even appropriate, emotion that can literally save their lives. We also need to teach them how to identify the real source of their fear when it arises and how to decide on the proper response.

This isn't easy territory, because sometimes the proper response is to get yourself out of the situation as fast as possible, while at other times, it is finding a way to control your fear in order to do the right thing. But unless we address the issue with our boys in a very supportive and open manner, we will leave them to the not-so-tender instruction of their peers.

Parents: Let your son know that we are all afraid at times and often for very good reasons. Help him to learn how to understand and properly respond to his fears, and never shame him for being afraid. Practice a few scenarios: If you feel afraid of a big boy, what should you do? If you are afraid of the math test next week, what should you do?

Teacher: Work to reduce classroom anxieties by openly talking about the challenges we all face in learning and expressing what we learn. Talk about strategies for deescalating the fear of oral reports, research papers, or other projects. Make fear discussable.

Compete without Competition

> *"One of my favorite things growing up was playing ping-pong with my dad. It was a regular evening routine, and I really cherished that time. When I was fourteen, I beat him for the first time and then he stopped playing me."*

Competition as a valuable element of childrearing has gone through a roller-coaster ride of acceptance, abhorrence, and more recently, back to grudging acceptance. From the time when young men were expected to be "honed through competitive sports," to the early days of the women's movement when competition was criticized as a ruthless tool of male domination, to more recent revelations that participation in competitive team sports can positively influence girls' self-esteem, the pendulum has swung back and forth.

Today, with a much more balanced view, we can see the obvious benefits of healthy competition: it can help our boys strive to improve; it can help teach them the value of teamwork, the joy of success and accomplishment, and the inevitability of failure. In short it can provide them with a balanced microcosm of life's experiences to learn from, but it can still be badly misused if the sole point of competition becomes winning.

From the sports parents who push their children to sacrifice everything to be "winners," to the weekend warriors who care more about beating their sons in whatever game they are playing than enjoying the excitement of playing, cutthroat competition teaches all the wrong lessons—the worst of them being that you are either a winner or a loser. Help your son realize that what matters, win or lose, is how you play the game.

Parents: Encourage your son's interest in competitive sports and participate as much as you can, but make sure he is getting the real benefits of competition by stressing the joy and excitement of playing and that he is improving without letting it become a do-or-die trial of his budding masculinity.

Teachers: Take time to play some cooperative games in which there aren't winners and losers to balance out the competitive experiences in most kids' lives.

Take Your Son to Work

"I grew up silently terrified of work. I saw my father go off to work every day, and he hated his job. Work seemed to me to be some kind of horrible punishment that was given to men when they grew up."

The women's movement created "Take Your Daughter to Work Day," and it has proven a very successful way to expose young girls to opportunities in the working world. We need to do the same for our boys, but for a very different purpose. Yes, it does help to expose them to working environments, but more importantly it provides the opportunity to demystify what can still seem to them a frightening future. Small boys do not yet have the resources to understand what meaningful work can be, but they already know that this is someday going to be their fate, and it can and often does fill them with foreboding. Seeing a functioning workplace in action can go a long way toward deflating their fears of a lifelong sentence.

Also, our sons rarely have the opportunity to observe us interacting with other adults in an atmosphere of mutual respect and teamwork. This in itself can go a long way toward broadening their perspective of the rich diversity of human interaction. Just getting to see men and women working together, seeing their parents surrounded by friendly colleagues, addressing problems together, sharing their pride in their visiting son can make our boys' worlds larger. Our world strains to make a boy's world smaller and smaller, and everything we can do to expand that world is important.

Parents: Take your sons to work with you. Don't wait for one day a year. Pick times when something vibrant and exciting is happening so they can experience work as what it should be and not what they fear it is. Then take time to show them around and introduce them to the best of your colleagues.

Teachers: Many businesses welcome visits from schoolchildren, so reach out into your community and try to set up regular field trips to broaden your students' exposure to the working world. Make sure you include trips to visit people who are passionate about what they do, so that the world of work isn't presented as all drudgery.

Support His Tenderness

"When I was seven, my parents had just moved to a new house across town, and I had to face third grade in a new school. I wasn't looking forward to it, but when I got there, I saw one of my best friends from the old school was in my class. I was so excited and relieved I ran across the room and hugged him and was immediately physically pulled apart and scolded by my new teacher. That was the beginning of one of the worst years in my life."

Every parent who has ever raised a boy knows that they not only have the capacity for great tenderness, but freely give of it when they are young: toward siblings, animals, parents, relatives, friends, and even complete strangers. But that outpouring of care and concern for others will be obliterated if we don't go out of our way to encourage it. For unfortunately, our cultural legacy is that tenderness is for girls, and boys who demonstrate tenderness are wimps or worse.

This is a poisonous and extremely damaging message, but it is one they will hear again and again as they are growing up. By the banal drivel of the entertainment industry, by adults who are immersed in foolish mythology about masculinity, and by peers who have already fallen victim to the lies, our sons are told that kindness and compassion, two essential human qualities, are for sissies.

Without our help, without our support, they have little hope of withstanding the relentless pressure. This is no small matter. Cut off from their natural tendency toward kindness, they will grow up at first pretending to be tough and uncaring, then gradually coming to believe it, and finally celebrating their cynicism as if it were a shining mark of independence. And all the while in the deep recesses of their hearts they will know that they have lost something important.

Parents: Celebrate their tenderness whenever it arises, and go out of your way to create opportunities for them to show their innate kindness. Instill in them the importance of small gestures of compassion, and let them experience for themselves how powerful and rewarding it can be.

Teachers: Teach the power and majesty of kindness. Have your class plan and organize a celebration of the annual Random Acts of KindnessTM week to let them see how they can be a part of a movement dedicated to returning compassion to an honored place in our lives.

Watch for Signs of Racism

"I went to a very integrated high school, which in retrospect gave me a much better picture of the world than I would have had, but unfortunately many of my memories of that time are of racial comments and put-downs the different groups used to throw around. Most of it wasn't really serious, but I'm ashamed to say I participated as well."

Racism is a complicated issue, but I believe that one of the reasons young boys get dragged into racism is that we raise them disconnected from their selves, their families, and their emotions. The resulting strong need to feel connected somewhere in their lives manifests itself in the worst ways and makes them susceptible to dysfunctional group psychology. Feelings of inadequacy and the need to belong can superficially be satisfied by "us" versus "them" dynamics.

In addition, historically boys have been taught and even rewarded to see others as objects worthy of hating and killing. Without the capacity for empathy and connection to their own feelings, boys can more easily depersonalize others, and thus are easy targets for racist thinking.

Rooted in ignorance and the absence of compassion, racism is an insidious disease that damages everyone who comes in contact with it. It is also, unfortunately, a prominent aspect of the world our children are growing into. In order to combat racism, we need to provide our sons with both the capacity for empathy and compassion and the experience of feeling a part of the incredible diversity of our world. Expose them to your friends from different ethnic backgrounds so they can feel the richness that all people bring to life. Talk about the kinds of differences that exist between people, and the care we should offer to all.

Parents: Listen carefully for any signs of racism, small comments, jokes, snickers, lack of respect. Intervene immediately and explain as clearly as possible how wrong it is. But also realize that it can be a sign that you need to do a better job of helping your boy feel good about himself and his connection to others.

Teachers: Make multicultural awareness a part of daily life in your classroom. Explore each person's ethnic background. Have an international market or fair.

Is the Internet Causing Problems for the Boy in Your Life?

A Pew Research study found in 2015 that 92 percent of teenagers said they spend time online every day; one in four described themselves as being on the internet "nearly constantly." Of course, like other young people, boys can socialize with existing friends and potentially connect with new ones in online spaces. But too much of the wrong kind of online experiences can leave them contending with a gaming habit, cyberbullying, and/or body image issues or other anxieties exacerbated by interactions in such contexts.

As the Social Media Research Association states, "Boys and girls...have differing perceptions of the amount of time they spend using various technologies. Girls are somewhat more likely than boys to say they spend too much time on social media (47 percent vs. 35 percent). By contrast, boys are roughly four times as likely [as girls are] to say they spend too much time playing video games (41 percent of boys and 11 percent of girls say this)." Girls are more likely to spend excessive time on social media, with an associated higher likelihood of depression and cyberbullying, but that doesn't mean boys are entirely in the clear. According to findings of the UK Millennium Cohort Study, which looked at more than ten thousand fourteen-year-olds, spending more hours scrolling through social media correlated to a higher risk of depression for all teenagers; the more hours spent engaging with social media, the greater the probability of depressed mood.

Too much time online, whether on social media or solo or multiplayer gaming, can become a real problem. As Cam Adair, founder of the group Game Quitters, an online recovery support community for people struggling with video game addictions, told the *Wall Street Journal*, ""The cycle works like this: Gamers develop a problem in high school, but they are able to get away with it. The transition to college is a different story; there's less parental supervision, more independence, more responsibilities, a change in their social environment, [and] more difficult classwork, and they experience an increase in stress. To deal with stress, they play video games, which causes them to get behind in class, which causes more stress, and they escape further into games to deal with it, perpetuating the problem. This creates a cycle of academic self-destruction."

Boys may also be significantly influenced by images they see on social media and can be drawn into comparing themselves to the idealized male physiques there, whether in posts or advertising. Some boys develop body image issues at as young an age as six to eight years old. With the number of perfectly staged and filtered images to be found online, it's no shock that some drift into unhealthy perspectives on their own bodies.

"How do we know if our son has a problem with gaming or other digital media?"

Here are some warning signs:

- Skipping meals or sleep: Is your son sleeping too long during the day? Is he losing weight? Check if signs like this are caused by too much time gaming or scrolling.

- Losing interest in school or other real-life activities: Has your son reduced the time he spends with his friends? Has he stopped engaging in extracurricular activities like sports or other hobbies he once enjoyed? In particular, teenage boys in high school should be getting ready for the shift to adult life, not regressing into a digital existence.

- **Aggressive reactions when challenged:** Some upset is natural when a boy is asked to interrupt gaming or decrease social media time, but if an angry response goes on a long time or is very intense, that can be a danger signal.

Of course, parents want to support their sons in keeping their amount of screen time balanced and engaging with online contexts safely. Here are some tips on how to do that:

- Consider setting up parental controls on your son's screen time. The major gaming platforms (Xbox, PlayStation, and Nintendo) all allow parents to set password-protected restrictions on gaming access by age and ratings, on how much screen time is allowed and when, and on whether a young person can make purchases. Some controls even let you turn your son's access on or off via a smartphone app, and others even give onscreen warnings when a young gamer is about to exceed the allotted time!

- Experts say it may be best not to allow kids to have gaming consoles—or even smartphones—in their bedrooms at night. Of course, if your son has no trouble managing screen time, it may be a good idea to relax this policy to some degree as he gets closer to leaving the nest so he can practice dealing with online temptations before he's on his own.

- The nonprofit Paul Anderson Youth Home advises, "Be present with your boys and create phone-free zones, such as dinner time or until homework is complete."

- Family therapist Dr. Lori Whatley of Atlanta, who specializes in digital device usage, suggests that parents create a digital detox for their teenagers, either before they depart for college and/or during vacations at home, with no videogames allowed. This time period can help your son's sleep patterns come back into balance, as well as building and solidifying real, live, in-person relationships. Thirty days is a good length of time if there is a need to develop a healthy new way of being to displace problematic habits.

When your son is actually engaged with a game and it's time to ask him to stop, tech-savvy gamer and father of two Dan Feierabend offers some useful insights:

> *Communicate when it's time to take a break, but let your kids finish the current round or match before insisting they stop playing.*

> *At times, your child may bargain for "just one more." If they're playing competitively online, it can be difficult to leave in the middle of a match. Their team may lose if they have to quit early, or they may even be penalized and suspended from further online play.*

> *If you allow your child to play online games, set rules ahead of time. Let them know that if you ask them to stop playing, they must stop right away or risk immediate loss of gaming privileges. Tell your child you understand that sometimes they can't just quit or pause, so you'll make a special allowance depending on the circumstances. It can be challenging to hold your ground, especially if your child gets emotional and tempers flare. But generally, a ten-minute heads-up should give your child time to finish a match.*

Stopbullying.gov provides some great steps to combat cyberbullying, which they define as "sending, posting, or sharing negative, harmful, false, or mean content... It can include sharing personal or private information about someone else causing embarrassment or humiliation. Some cyberbullying crosses the line into unlawful or criminal behavior":

- Find out from your son what his favorite game is, then sit in and watch him play it. Ask questions so you can better understand how the game play works—or even try it!

- When your son is online, make it a habit to occasionally check in with him and ask about who his fellow players are. This can keep you in the loop, as well as letting your son know that even though you are giving him space, you're still involved.

- Make it very clear to your son that caution is necessary when interacting with strangers online, including in multiplayer games—and be sure to go over how important it is not to give out any personal information without appropriate safeguards. This includes his last name, the name of his school, email and physical addresses, and phone numbers. And explain to him that he *must* get your explicit permission before accepting any gifts or rewards from any person online. Predators use giving gifts as a simple way to build trust with a targeted child; it isn't hard to give digital gifts like game resource codes, loot boxes, or even cash cards.

- It is also important to let him know that you won't tolerate him verbalizing abusive insults toward others, not even in the heat of game play.

For more information, check out their wide-ranging online article: www.stopbullying.gov/cyberbullying/kids-on-social-media-and-gaming

CHAPTER 6

Creating a New Model of Manhood

This is the shortest chapter of the book, not because it is less important, but because it deals with something that is yet to emerge—a new model of masculinity. We can encourage and support boys in their efforts to hone their emotional intelligence and live connected to their hearts, but they can't do that fully unless the very notion of being a man changes. Even today, the hallmark of manhood touted on TV and elsewhere is a football-watching emotional idiot. Just last night on TV, there was a guy in the midst of a breakup saying to a friend, "I think I feel something, like emotions. Have you ever felt emotions?"

As parents and concerned caregivers, we are the midwives of this extraordinary transformation. But ultimately the new definition of manhood will emerge from the minds and hearts of our sons as they grow and develop.

The largest responsibility for the creation of a new definition of manhood is theirs to discover, to experience, to experiment with, and to refine. What we can do is open the discussion, support them in their efforts, and create a strong support system around them that reinforces the benefits of emotional expression and deep interpersonal connection.

Talk about the Mixed Messages of Manhood

> *"Looking back at when I was growing up, I realize that the main question that I struggled with for most of my childhood was, 'What exactly does it mean to be a man?' I never actually articulated that question, and I certainly never asked anyone. I just kept trying to pick up clues wherever I could find them."*

It's a mark of how blinded we are as a culture that the core question our sons have to struggle with is not even a topic of conversation. What is clear is that our definition of a good man is in a tumultuous and confusing transition. The old models, from knights in shining armor to John Wayne, still hold some attraction but are clearly one-dimensional and inadequate. The new models that appear out of the "Sensitive New Age Guy" sitcom portrayal of fumbling manhood offer half-baked alternatives riddled with their own inadequacies.

So how do we help our sons deal with this heavy burden? How can they possibly know what direction they need to head if no one is willing to admit the question is out there?

By talking about it. By shining the bright light of reason on this murky and frightening issue. We may not have the answers yet; we may not be able to articulate exactly how a man should be strong without violence and anger, sensitive and compassionate without losing self-focus, and generous without giving himself away. We may not have a clear picture of how we want the pieces to fit together, but if there is a better topic of ongoing conversation, I can't think of it.

Parents: Let your son know that he is an important part of an extraordinary process—the redefinition of what it is to be a man—and regularly invite his active participation in exploring what that definition should be.

Teachers: This is a great topic for classwork. We are in the midst of a historic cultural transition. Why leave it to historians to look back years from now and tell us what we did? Invite all your budding social theorists to dive in and create their own pictures of what a man should be.

Read History through New Eyes

> *"One of my favorite memories was reading the same books as my father and talking about them. It was a tradition we accidentally started when he told me that The Once and Future King was one of his favorite books, so we both decided to read it."*

We are a product of our history, and that is more true in how we perceive our roles as men and women than we might care to admit. Gender roles have been handed down for generation after generation. Often these roles were rooted in very practical and useful historical divisions of labor and only became constricting later, when the circumstances that gave rise to them changed but the role separations continued.

One of the most enjoyable ways to explore this history and unravel the reasons that made sense and the reasons that no longer make sense is to go back in time with your children and explore the world of gender roles. Expose them to stories of other cultures in which things were divided up differently. Give your children the gift of perspective and the challenge of imagination. Use history to open their minds to what the present is and what the future should be.

Parents: Through history books, historical fiction, historical movies, and active imagination, try to capture with your sons what life must have been like in prehistoric times, when people lived in small tribes, at the dawn of agriculture, during the rise of the first great civilizations on Earth. Talk about life expectancies, the dangers and challenges of each period, and wonder with your sons about why men and women assumed different roles at different times. Have your children imagine what they would have felt like living during various points in history and what they would have dreamed of doing. Then bring them closer and closer to our time and examine how the roles have changed; imagine what the future might hold and what changes they think should be made.

Teachers: Include the topic of gender roles in as many areas of the curriculum as you can. How many math story problems are about boys and how many about girls? Find old textbooks and compare then and now. How many women scientists are included now compared to texts thirty years ago?

Be Aware of the Peter Pan Syndrome

"When I look back at my life, I realize that I must have spent a good decade and a half, starting in my mid-teens, trying desperately to avoid growing up. No matter how I looked at it, being a man carried so much frightening baggage that it just didn't seem worth the effort."

It is small wonder that so many adolescents and young men are wildly ambivalent about leaving childhood behind. We expect men to be strong, to take responsibility, to be accomplished in whatever they do, to measure themselves by how they succeed financially, to provide for and protect their families, and never to show weakness or overt emotion. Yes, things are beginning to change, but expectations are still there. This kind of change takes generations, not decades.

The truth is our boys are rightfully frightened by what they often see as a landscape of loneliness, hard work, and sacrifice. In their adolescence and young adulthood our boys reach the second crisis point in their lives, and we need to be there with them if they are to have any chance of emerging into rich and full lives. They need to hear from us that there are other paths, other options, that they can and should look at growing up not only as an exciting adventure, but one that can bring them more deeply in touch with their true selves.

This is a pivotal moment in their lives and one fraught with hesitation, uncertainty, and fear. It is a time when they need every bit of our compassion, insight, wisdom, and guidance. It is also unfortunately a time when most parents tend to back away, simply because the intensity of the challenge is so great, and all too often the groundwork for a relationship characterized by wide-open, honest, and empathetic communication has somehow been let slide.

Parents: No matter what you have done right or wrong up to this point, your son desperately needs you in his teens and twenties. What he needs more than anything is your understanding and compassion. Open your heart as wide as possible and let him know that you know how stressful this time is and that you will be there for him no matter what.

Teachers: Encourage students to explore the many ways they can learn life's lessons after high school—college, traveling, pursuing interests in the arts, community service. Each offers ways to gather knowledge about the world and to discover more about the lives they want to lead.

Encourage Close Friendships

"My son's friends used to congregate at our house. At times it was a real nuisance (particularly when they got older and were staying up late noisily watching movies), but most of the time, it was pure high-energy joy. As the years went by, I noticed that my son and I always felt closer and talked more freely right after visits from the gang. I think in an odd way my acceptance of and respect for his friends reminded him how much I love him."

It is hard to imagine how lonely and isolated growing up male can be. My own memories seem to be wrapped in layer after layer of gauze, as if to protect me from the raw wounds of those years. Sometimes it seems like everything is working against you: the continuous barrage of messages about all the things you are supposed to be but are in fact incapable of being; the constant competition, teasing, and taunting by your equally insecure peers, who somehow think that by putting you down it raises them up; the painful emotional distance that suddenly forms between you and your parents.

During times like that, the more fortunate of us had someone to turn to, a real friend, a friend who wasn't afraid to drop the defenses and games, a friend you talk to (even if it was in weird teenage boyspeak) about anything and everything. For many boys, this kind of friend was and is literally a lifeline, sometimes the only lifeline that keeps them connected to the world outside their own heads. When these people show up in our sons' lives, they should be celebrated and honored for the extraordinary gifts they bring.

Parents: Treat your son's friends as if they were your own. Love them, cherish them, make them welcome and comfortable in your home, because what they mean to your son is immeasurable.

> **Teachers:** Help kids expand their friendships by offering
> opportunities to work collaboratively in intellectual pursuits.

Create a Circle of Men

*"Some of my best memories of my father revolve around the
evenings a special group of his oldest friends would come
over and play poker. I was the fly on the wall, hanging
around to get more chips or beer when needed, and I got to
listen to all these great stories and conversations about what
happened to this guy and 'Remember when we...' It was one
of my only windows into my father's life."*

In tribal cultures, the men initiate boys into the man's
world with the tribe by including them in gatherings where
stories are shared, plans are made, and responsibilities
are allocated. Those days are long gone for most of us, but
we need to find new ways to let our sons into our lives, to
give them the chance to see us in all facets of who we are.
One of the best ways to accomplish this is to get together
with your own friends on a regular basis and make it an
informal father-son gathering.

If we are to give our boys a solid foundation upon which
to build their own identities as men, the more depth and

experience we can expose them to the better. Creating your own circle of men is a powerful way to enrich your son's understanding of the issues that will confront him in his life.

Parents: The key is to set up such a circle with plenty of room for fun and open enough to encompass storytelling and discussion on any topic (this precludes the Sunday football game, which serves its own purpose but doesn't leave enough room for wide-ranging discussion). A monthly "guys only" barbecue or overnight fishing and camping trip would do nicely. Even a rotating weekly card game or book discussion group will work. Anything you can think of that would create space for letting go of the daily grind, softening up on the "Dad as boss" role, and instead invite in the world of wonder and curiosity.

Teachers: Create occasions where boys can hang out with their male teachers. A community skating party or picnic could allow boys to see and talk to these important "guys" on a casual basis.

Be Explicit about Social Expectations

"There is this weird television ad I've seen a couple times that has kids telling the camera their 'life dreams.' The one I remember was a young boy saying something like, 'I want to grow up, claw my way to middle management, and then be laid off in a corporate downsizing.'"

If we are going to help our sons create their own visions for the new man, we first have to help them identify the culturally embedded expectations that litter the landscape of a young boy's life. The best way to deal with things that hide in the shadows is to drag them out into the light and pick them apart until we understand the how and why of their existence.

Be strong, get good grades, go to a good university, graduate in the top of your class, get a good job, get married, have kids. How often is this mantra or a variation on it repeated in a young boy's life, and yet how often do we stop to ask and seriously address the question "Why?" When we fail to take this step, we leave our advice out there as an end in itself, as if this were the path to salvation instead of just as likely a path to being a downsized middle manager.

Expectations, whether socially induced or our own personal expectations (as in "When you grow up you can be a lawyer like your dad") certainly allow for possible paths, but they can weigh very heavily on a small boy's shoulders. How many people do you know who did what was expected of them and are now stuck in miserable situations? If we are to prepare our sons to follow their own unique paths, we first need to dismantle all the blocks that have caused them to believe that they should live by what others expect of them.

Parents: Ask your son what he thinks is expected of him in life. Then articulate your own expectations.

Teachers: Begin an exploration of expectations. Have students write down what they think their parents expect of them. Make it a homework assignment for families to discuss these writings. Then, later in class, talk about how the kids' assumptions were accurate and how they were not.

Initiate Him into Manhood

"Watching my son grow up got me to thinking about my own childhood. I tried to think about when I stopped being a boy and became a man, but there was nothing there to mark the transition. I was a boy, and then many years later, everyone assumed I was a man, but inside, I wasn't even sure what that meant."

When does a boy become a man? Is it when he gets his driver's license? The first time he needs to shave? His first wet dream or when that first frightening pubic hair appears? When he hits twenty-one?

If you are like me, even raising the question creates discomfort. The truth is as a society we no longer have an answer, and that in itself is deeply disturbing. How are our sons supposed to find their way into healthy manhood when we can't even tell them when it begins, much less mark this extraordinary moment with a ritual of celebration?

Being a woman is something we can define. When our daughter experienced her first menses, and when her body physically develops into a more mature form, she has crossed the threshold from being a little girl to being a young woman. There is no threshold for boys. What it means to become a man is left in an unarticulated gray zone that leads to confusion, insecurity, and just as often inappropriate efforts by young men to prove to themselves and their peers that they are men. The very absence of acknowledgment and initiation can set off a lifetime of trying to prove manhood instead of growing into manhood as fully as possible.

Parents: Since we have no clear demarcation, make up one you are comfortable with and then celebrate that occasion as openly, proudly, and solemnly as possible. Give your son the honor and certainty of knowing that he has become a young man. Take the occasion to articulate your belief in the wonderful man he will become.

Teachers: One way to introduce this subject is through cross-cultural comparisons. Discuss initiation rites and what they mean to different cultures.

Help Him Find His Passion

> *"When I was in high school, I used to write all the time in a big tattered notebook. Many years later, my father handed me the notebook telling me he had found it when he was cleaning out the storage area. He apologized for reading it, then told me he was really impressed with lots of what I had written, but felt badly that he had never even known I had this private world all those years."*

Our job in life is to find the thing that we are passionate about and bring it into the center of our lives. That is difficult enough to do under the best of circumstances but can be near impossible when the very resources we need to discover and tap into our passions are systematically denied to us.

As parents, we all want our children to lead happy, fulfilling lives. Yes, we want them to be successful and comfortable but not at the expense of their happiness. Yet that goal can never be reached unless and until they discover the deepest parts of themselves, where their passion and purpose reside.

We can help as parents, both by encouraging and supporting them in their exploration of their emotional and spiritual selves and by paying close attention to the things that they become excited about. Children often move through phases of interest, trying out one thing or another and then suddenly losing interest. Don't let this pattern lull you into complacency. Get engaged in each and every interest they develop. Help them explore it, support their interest, encourage their experimentation, kindle their enthusiasm. But be careful not to appropriate it yourself or assume that because he loves photography today, he is going to be a photographer. That kind of pressure can cause kids to withdraw altogether.

Parents: Ask your son today what he's most excited about and engage in a conversation about it.

Teachers: With so many required topics to teach, we rarely leave room for students to pursue their own intellectual interests. Have students make and keep ongoing lists of interesting questions, and periodically allow them time to investigate something they are passionate about.

Teach Listening Skills

"My son had gotten in trouble at school for hitting another boy, and after talking to him for about ten minutes and watching him get increasingly agitated, I asked him what I had just said. He replied, 'You think I'm bad!' which was of course not at all what I had said."

We think that because we can hear, we are all listening. How far from the truth! Real listening is a skill that far too many of us, adults and children, have never mastered.

As a generalization, men tend to have more trouble with this than women; real listening is an aspect of empathy, which we have not been well trained in. We get so caught up in our own feelings and fears, and by trying to deflect criticism, we forget completely to listen to what is being said. This is a very real danger with our sons because they already feel enormous pressure to be good, to be perfect, to be strong, and to be accomplished; so any time they fail, they are scared to death they will lose your love and respect completely—that you will simply conclude they are bad.

One of the best ways to teach them how to listen is simply to have them repeat back to you in their own words what you said. It is particularly effective if you do the same first for them, because it makes it seem more evenhanded and not just a stupid parent trick. This is important, because they aren't always as skilled as we might want them to be at articulating what they feel, and it sometimes comes out wrong. By repeating it back to them, they get a chance to revise. It also comes in handy because we aren't always that good at listening to them either.

Parents: Teach listening skills by reporting to each other your versions of the conversation: what I heard you say was... The first time you try this exercise, it might seem like a comical version of the old "telephone" game in which something gets passed along a string of people and comes out all garbled at the end. Yet with practice, it becomes easier and easier and an awful lot of miscommunication disappears.

Teachers: Help your students learn what helps them listen well. For some, eye contact with the person they are listening to is essential; for others it gets in the way of hearing what is being said. Some people listen best while moving; others need to take notes or make a diagram. Support your students' understanding that people need different things to learn well. To learn more about this, read Dawna Markova's and Anne Powell's two books, *How Your Child Is Smart* and *Learning Unlimited*.

Cultivate Consideration

"My daughter always volunteers to help with dinner, whereas it's always a struggle to get my son to even do his assigned chores. I don't know what to do about it!"

It's yet another gender stereotype: Girls tend to be more helpful and more considerate of others than boys. One theory says that because girls value connection more than boys, they cultivate the qualities that help them to stay close, including empathy and social helpfulness. Whether that is innate or culturally determined, there's no rule that says boys should not also be considerate and caring toward others.

Consideration is a mild form of empathy. It requires thinking about what another person might need in any given moment and offering to help. The more our boys are connected to their own feelings, the more they will be able to recognize that others have feelings too, and the more consideration will be a natural part of their repertoire.

But we can help things along by reinforcing the consideration they do exhibit: "That was nice that you are letting Marcy play with the bike now." And we can teach them overtly to think about others and offer their assistance: "Do you think Grandma might need some help getting the turkey on the table?" The more we do both, the more they will tune in to this important component of emotional intelligence.

Parents: Don't allow gender stereotyping to cause you to neglect passing on this crucial emotional skill. Being considerate is something boys *and* girls can learn.

Teachers: Point out good examples of consideration in the classroom. Help students learn to explore and take care of the needs of others. "Consideration Captain" could even be a weekly job—to notice when someone needs a helping hand.

Encourage Intimacy, Even If It's Covert

"When I was in high school, my mom wanted to take this dance class, but my father refused to go with her, so she started bugging me to go. I resisted but finally agreed to give it a try when she told me girls love a good dancer. It turned out to be a great experience. I'd never seen my mother giggling and having so much fun, and it just felt great to be a part of it."

Due to all of the silly messages our boys receive growing up, there is almost always a time when they start to pull back. All the things you used to do with your son that kept you connected both physically and emotionally, the hugging, cuddling, and wide-open communication, suddenly don't seem comfortable to him. When this happens, our challenge is to bridge that moment of uncertainty in a way that is easy and inviting and does not trigger his confusion even further.

The pressures of our culture are going to pull your son away from you, and you need to become terribly clever at devising ways to keep him close. If he is emotionally distancing himself, devise ways to create quiet time together where opportunities to reestablish that connection can emerge. Read the same book he's reading and find time to discuss it with him. Ask for his help on a project that you are really interested in (like planning and executing new tile for the bathroom, building a doghouse, anything that can get you both together). Devise code words that mean "I love you" that won't embarrass him in front of his friends, like "Watch out for purple alligators!" Whatever you do, don't just let him drift off.

Parents: If he has pulled away physically, try exaggerated playful (and thus not terribly embarrassing) hugs. Interrupt watching a Sunday football game by demonstrating (on him) the proper way to tackle Barry Sanders; if he likes to wrestle, all the better. If that doesn't work, try the lingering pat on the back or any other ruse you can think of to make contact in a way that is not embarrassing.

Teachers: Discover small ways to physically show admiration and respect for your students. Maybe a special handshake when they've done a great job or need a little boost.

Get Him a Pet

"I had a dog from the time I was five. She was my closest friend. She died when I was fifteen, and I cried like a baby."

The image of a boy and his dog is a heart-filled one, and rightly so. Having a pet, particularly a dog or cat, is a wonderful experience for any child. It teaches responsibility, steadfastness, and loyalty, and most important to the topic of this book, it gives a boy the chance to learn nurturance, lovingly caring for a being beside oneself.

The animal-child bond is so significant that studies have shown that cruelty toward animals is an early indication of violence in adolescence. That makes sense—children who learn to be loving toward animals will be loving toward people, and those who learn cruelty will be cruel.

But a pet, particularly a dog, provides something else a boy needs: someone who loves him unconditionally. That kind of love and devotion comes in handy on those days when he feels life is hard and the whole world is against him.

Parents: Get him a warm, wiggly puppy or kitten. If that's impossible, how about a rabbit or a hamster? There's something about furriness that really helps with the emotional bonding you're trying to support. And if he's old enough, make sure *he* does the work!

Teachers: A classroom pet can bring the element of nurturing into the school day. If a real rabbit or hamster won't work, for younger kids, have a stuffed soft mascot who can go home with each child and have adventures over the weekend.

Create and Carry On Traditions

"When I was very little, my father used to get up early on Saturday and take me out for a leisurely breakfast and walk in order to give my mom a chance to sleep in. With minor interruptions, we have kept up that ritual now for over twenty years."

In the "old days," family, clan, tribal, or village rituals were a central part of growing up. Indeed, it was through these traditions that children became meaningfully rooted as a part of the group and learned their place within it. It was a way to teach the importance of continuity and connection, to initiate children into the deeper fabric of life, and to provide a strong experience of identity.

In modern culture, the world of ritual has been stripped down to a handful of national or religious holidays which all too often have been diluted of meaning by commercialization and our own lack of understanding of their importance. We live today in a world bereft of meaningful traditions, and that is a tragedy that has a great impact on our children.

It is difficult enough to raise self-aware and connected boys in a culture where the forces of socialization are already trying to pull them away; without meaningful traditions to give them something to hold onto, the task becomes even harder. We need to create as many regular opportunities to get away from the normal flow of day-to-day life and move instead into sacred time together, time where the purpose is to honor and celebrate the deeper connection between us. Create your own traditions, and don't let anything get in their way.

Parents: Make the traditions you observe meaningful by seeing holidays as more than excuses to buy presents or go to the amusement park. Reinject them with the meaning they are supposed to carry. Invent new traditions that can provide an anchor for your son, be it a regular breakfast, a monthly walk in the woods, semi-annual wilderness camping trips, or an evening out together each month—whatever feels right for you and your son. Stick with it and imbue it with that special quality of time apart.

Teachers: Classrooms are very much like a large and sometimes unwieldy family. Creating class traditions that give students an opportunity to experience themselves doing something meaningful as a part of a group can ground them and remind them of the fuller aspects of their lives. Rituals for beginning or ending the day can foster a sense of belonging.

Have Family Field Trips

> *"The times I've remembered best from my childhood were always the family vacations. They sit in my memories like shining jewels."*

Traditionally, work has had priority over family in men's lives. If we want to teach our sons the value of strong emotional connection, we need to place the family at the center of our own lives. One of the simplest ways to show how special your family is to you is to do something special together. It's obvious, but in the increasingly rapid pace of our lives, we can easily forget to take the time to do the obvious. When they are very young, we tend to do more of this—going to the park, the zoo, the amusement park—but if we are really honest, our motivation is more often than not a way to occupy their time rather than an opportunity to spend time together.

Reorient the sense of priority and try to find things that create opportunities for interaction. Make it a regular part of your planning to schedule in special occasions for the whole family. Show by your actions that being together is important.

> **Parents:** Family vacations work great, especially if they are not
> overly packed with "get here, see this, do that." The traditional
> day at the ballpark is great for baseball lovers since the pace of
> the game itself is conducive to plenty of rambling conversation.
> Take your family on a business trip with you when you can
> schedule in an extra overnight (save the company money
> by staying over through Saturday). Or take nature hikes and
> explore together the natural history of your region.
>
> **Teachers:** Field trips often do wonders for classroom bonding.
> Consider a special trip that students can look forward to even
> before they get to your class, such as a camping trip you take
> each fall.

Schedule Family Dinners

> *"I remember watching The Waltons on TV, everyone sitting
> around the dinner table being nice to each other. At my house,
> the kitchen was more like a fast-food stopover. Occasionally
> you'd end up running into each other, but it was always
> in passing."*

Study after study has shown that the best protection
against virtually all manner of adolescent pitfalls, from
drinking and drugs to gangs and juvenile delinquency,
is a close family connection. Isn't it wonderful when

all the studies agree with what our common sense already tells us?

The challenge here is to keep that close family tie in the midst of all the pressures pulling us apart, and the first step is to acknowledge that it isn't all that simple. Parents of young boys are frequently in the most hectic phase of their own lives. With nurturing their marriage, keeping in touch with friends, taking care of all the material issues of house and home and family, and investing time building a career identity, it's easy not only to let the kids head off on their own, but to be relieved when they do.

Young boys have their own reasons for pulling out of the family orbit, ranging from the appropriate, like differing interests and the need to have some space for their own identity to grow, to the inappropriate, like unresolved anger and resentment as well as peer pressure to "be an independent man." The net result is that if you don't make a serious effort to hold the center and keep everyone safely within the family's orbit, it isn't going to happen.

One way to do this is to reestablish the good old-fashioned tradition of eating together. It's amazing how many of us have almost completely given up on family dinners, but despite the obstacles (including differing schedules and taste buds), it is well worth the effort even if you have to compromise on the number of family dinner nights per week. Remember, you don't want this to be punishment; it should be a collective opportunity to reconnect in a judgment-free environment.

Parents: If you don't already, plan for at least one family meal a week, attendance mandatory. Expand the opportunity for connection by rotating cooking and cooking assistant positions throughout the family. Then when you sit down, focus on the positive; don't use this precious time to complain, criticize, or hand out advice unless it is requested.

Teachers: Eating together can also be fun at school. Invite a few students to lunch once a week. Get to know them a little better during this more casual time.

Articulate Your Values

"My father died when I was eight. I no longer know whether my memory of him is accurate or not, but what I do remember was the way he always seemed to be completely focused on whatever he was doing. It is my secret yardstick to the way I want to live my life."

If we want our sons to live lives full of purpose and meaning, the very best thing we can do is make an example of our own lives for them. In our fast-paced, harried world, the temptation is always there to cut corners, to get to the point, to get to the result, to cross things off our lists as quickly as possible and move on to the next task. In the process we become sleepwalkers, moving through our lives without life moving through us.

What is our purpose? What values guide us through the course of our own lives? The more we examine these things for ourselves and the more we discuss them with our children, the more we offer them a worthwhile model for living. If we want more for our son than a life on the corporate treadmill, we need to articulate and demonstrate how one navigates through life's events using his or her values.

The truth is, at some level we are all living our values; we just haven't examined them. But our choices reveal what's important to us: earning a six-figure salary; having a beautiful home; making a difference; creating a close family. We each hold some core value. Take some time to think about yours and talk about it with your family.

Parents: One way to get at your core value is to play this game—you can even try this with older kids. Pretend it is the end of your life and God is going to ask you one question about how you've lived. What question will it be?

Teachers: The decision to become a teacher is rarely made lightly. Let your students know what deep values undergird your choice of profession. They can learn from your example and commitment.

Connect Him to the Divine

"I went to church every Sunday with my family; but it really wasn't anything I thought about, it was just something we did. I'd listen to the sermons, sing the hymns, and repeat back along with everyone else, but that was it. It was like pizza on Friday and hot dogs and baseball on Saturday."

We have a saying: "Never discuss religion or politics." Why? Because they are deep, complex subjects about which each of us has our own strong opinions and so to "get along," we avoid them. But avoiding talking about our spiritual natures can be a crippling loss for our children. How can we possibly expect them to live their lives to the fullest if we hold back the very essence of who they are—their connection to the divine?

We spend incredible amounts of time and energy preparing our children to be successful and accomplished. We send them to the best schools, help them with their homework, and worry with them over emotional issues, but far too often we neglect the very foundation of their lives—their spiritual selves. Life is so much more than successfully handling the material and emotional issues that arise. Life has meaning and purpose; each of us exists uniquely within the greater web of life to find and walk our own path in connection with and support of the greater whole.

To prepare our children for this role, we need to share with them our own deepest spiritual feelings and beliefs. We need to open the doors to this extraordinary world of depth and beauty so that they can begin to get their bearings, see their part in the grand design, and take comfort in a connection to something so much greater than their individual lives.

Parents: We tend to raise our sons more than our daughters in a spiritual vacuum, almost as if we unconsciously believe that their job is to deal with the world and that is tough enough. Give your sons the benefits of your beliefs; encourage them to think and imagine what their greater spiritual purpose might be.

Teachers: Help kids understand that the subjects you study together are often stories of people pursuing their purpose in life—scientists, explorers, artists. Invite them to consider what story they would want told about them in a hundred years. What does that tell them about their life purpose?

Afterword

by Jeanne and Don Elium authors of *Raising a Son: Parents and the Making of a Healthy Man*

In the mid-1980s, when our son was very young, I was involved with a small revolution called the mythopoetic men's movement. Through the inspiration and guidance of poet Robert Bly, ritualist Shepherd Bliss, and drummer Bruce Silverman, men were coming together to explore what it meant to be a man. They met in homes, churches, the woods, and great halls to drum, recite poetry, sing, and share their unique and often painful experiences of growing up male in our modern culture. As a woman, I was privileged to observe and participate as a ritualist in this exciting phenomenon. I was stunned to perceive the grief men felt about their missed relationships with their fathers and their rage at their mothers who had tried to compensate for the loss. And they lamented their own resulting lack of fathering skills. I heard the fear and shame that some men experienced as boys since they were expected to fight at school simply because they were male. I felt the guilt that many men shared at being a part of the patriarchy and therefore blamed for all the evil and wrongdoing in our world. I witnessed the tenderness and attention that the men shared with each other as they revealed their deepest feelings. I was moved by their struggle to reach into their hearts to unearth what had been hidden there for so long. I was also struck by how difficult it was for these men to access their emotions and put them out there for others to hear. How unlike most women I knew. The men seemed to be trying to speak a new language, foreign and resistant.

My experiences made me fearful for our own small son, still so innocent and free of male stereotyping. Could we guide him to grow up proud of his masculine inheritance in spite of the skewed cultural biases these men in the men's movement railed against? Could he become the kind of man in touch with his masculine soul—strong yet kind; sensitive to his own feelings as well as to others around him, yet able to make decisions and take action; life-affirming rather than life-destroying? We looked for help and support on the shelves of our local bookstores but found no guides about nurturing the unique needs of boys. We felt that surely other parents must share our concern, so we wrote our first parenting book on raising sons.

Since then we have hoped and prayed that others will
join us in creating new models of manhood and parenting
guides to help our sons become who they truly are: whole
human beings capable of responding with both heads
and hearts. Our prayers have been answered in the many
recent books on raising boys, and especially in Will
Glennon's *Nurturing Boys*. His simple, straightforward
definitions of the problems facing parents, teachers, and
boys and his practical solutions help us all find our way
through the often-bewildering maze that lies between the
limiting cultural stereotypes and the full potential of the
human male.

There is a story from the days of Theseus of Athens,
Greece, about Procrustes, a marauder who oppressed
the country by attacking travelers as they journeyed on
the road to Athens. He had an iron bedstead onto which
he tied all travelers who fell into his hands. If they were
shorter than the bed, he stretched their limbs to make
them fit; if they were longer than the bed, he lopped off a
portion of their bodies.

This book challenges us all to explore our own emotional
intelligence, to uncover and overcome our limiting
understanding of how a boy or man should be, should act,
should believe. The ideas that men and boys should not
cry, should not feel pain, should not share their innermost
feelings, and should never be afraid put them on the bed

of Procrustes and either stretch them or cut off crucial parts of them to fit our cultural masculine roles. In the end we cripple our sons and render them incapable of being truly themselves and unable to respond to the needs of a suffering world. By guiding us to nurture our sons' emotional intelligence, Will Glennon frees us all to be who we truly are.

Acknowledgments

A big thank you to Jo Beaton, who persevered through months of physical pain to compile the research that allowed me to write this book. Much love and thanks also to Daphne Rose Kingma, who has been so integrally a part of my journey that I can no longer tell which thoughts and ideas, which words and expressions, are hers and which are mine. Thanks also to Dawna Markova for breaking down the boundaries that so easily hem in our thoughts, to Andy Bryner for so fearlessly existing on the frontier of maleness, and to Anne R. Powell for providing the insight and practical advice that I hope will make this a useful tool for teachers.

My deepest gratitude to the hundreds of parents and children whose generosity with their time, their stories, and their hearts has so richly informed every word of this book.

To my father, William Glennon, a debt of gratitude that can never be paid for the depth of his love, his unflagging commitment to allowing me to become myself, and the enormous generosity of his spirit. And finally, to my son, Damian, whose beautiful and pure spirit cracked my heart wide open, who has had to suffer through all my stumblings and mistakes and has still emerged as an extraordinary young man. It is to him I owe any kernels of insight and wisdom that may appear in this book.

About the Author

Will Glennon had an eclectic career as a journalist, successful businessman, appellate attorney, author, and founder of the Random Acts of Kindness Foundation, the World Kindness Movement, and an effort to spread the exchange student experience to millions of children through the use of digital technology. He traveled extensively but found his most rewarding calling at home as a father and a grandfather.

mango

Mango Publishing, established in 2014, publishes an eclectic list of books by diverse authors—both new and established voices—on topics ranging from business, personal growth, women's empowerment, LGBTQ studies, health, and spirituality to history, popular culture, time management, decluttering, lifestyle, mental wellness, aging, and sustainable living. We were recently named 2019's #1 fastest growing independent publisher by Publishers Weekly. Our success is driven by our main goal, which is to publish high quality books that will entertain readers as well as make a positive difference in their lives.

Our readers are our most important resource; we value your input, suggestions, and ideas. We'd love to hear from you—after all, we are publishing books for you!

Please stay in touch with us and follow us at:

Facebook: Mango Publishing
Twitter: @MangoPublishing
Instagram: @MangoPublishing
LinkedIn: Mango Publishing
Pinterest: Mango Publishing

Sign up for our newsletter at www.mangopublishinggroup.com and receive a free book!

Join us on Mango's journey to reinvent publishing, one book at a time.

9 781642 503708